PRAISE

"Reading *Chickens One Day, Feathers the Next* is like meeting an old friend, not simply because it is so richly companionable, but because you won't want to say goodbye. Wandering through these essays is like dipping into a life more varied and richly felt: experiences you've never had recollected with a sensitivity and insight you only hope you'd feel. You'll want to read it slowly, but you won't be able to. Before you know it, you'll find yourself at the end: lost, alone, feeling oddly bereft. And you'll discover perhaps the most appealing thing about this compulsively readable book: you can always read it again."
D. K. SMITH, AUTHOR, *BUNNY*

"In this collection of essays, Wise defines his life with coming and going of dogs and horses, perhaps even more than the ebb and flow of women. These essays comprise deeply personal, revealing stories about coming of age, loss of innocence, boyhood larks turning amiss, bad acts going unpunished, and sublime days ruined and ruined days somehow redeemed. Wise views life with a self-deprecating, yet wry, down-home sense of humor, and an ear keenly attuned to the vagaries of the human condition."
SUANNE SCHAFER, AUTHOR, *A DIFFERENT KIND OF FIRE*

"Guinotte Wise's essay collection is a rollicking Harley Davidson ride down a fascinating and vibrant Route 66 of American culture. Vietnam, jazz, art, advertising, horses, publishing—it's all here. Wise embraces his subjects with gusto, humor, and the full-throated awe of a writer who has lived one hell of a life. If you love the late Jim Harrison's work, you'll want to read Wise."
WHITNEY TERRELL, AUTHOR, *THE GOOD LIEUTENANT*

ABOUT THE AUTHOR

Guinotte Wise writes and welds steel sculpture on a farm in Resume Speed, Kansas. His short story collection *Night Train, Cold Beer* won publication by a university press and enough money to fix the soffits. Five more books since. A five-time Pushcart nominee, his fiction and poetry have been published in numerous literary journals, including *Atticus, The MacGuffin, Santa Fe Writers Project, Rattle,* and *The American Journal of Poetry*. His wife has an honest job in the city and drives one hundred miles a day to keep it.

www.wisesculpture.com

Guinotte Wise

CHICKENS ONE DAY, FEATHERS THE NEXT

www.vineleavespress.com

Chickens One Day, Feathers the Next
Copyright © 2022 Guinotte Wise
All rights reserved.

Print Edition
ISBN: 978-618-86002-6-3
Published by Vine Leaves Press in Greece 2022

No parts of this publication may be reproduced, stored in a retrieval system, or transmitted in any form or by any means, electronic, mechanical, photocopying, recording, or otherwise, without the prior written permission of the copyright owner.

This book is sold subject to the condition that it shall not, by way of trade or otherwise, be lent, resold, hired out, or otherwise circulated without the publisher's prior consent in any form of binding or cover other than that in which it is published and without a similar condition including this condition being imposed on the subsequent purchaser. Under no circumstances may any part of this book be photocopied for resale.

Cover design by Jessica Bell
Interior design by Amie McCracken

A catalogue record of this work is available from The National Library of Greece.

For Freddie, who gets me going and keeps me going.

"My life was the best omelette you could make with a chainsaw."

Thomas McGuane

CONTENTS

Foreword - 13

The Horse Worrier - 17

Knucklehead - 39

The Unnaturalist - 49

Publishers Never Call - 57

The Mangled Emmy - 61

An Overdue Love Letter to Tensas Parish - 65

Chickens One Day, Feathers the Next - 77

It's a Tulsa Kind of Day ... - 81

Racism by Default - 93

Rejections: Bugs On the Windshield - 101

The Unknown Writer - 105

They're Still Stealing van Goghs - 109

Visualizing: Not a Woo-Woo science - 117

Welterweights - 123

Why I Write - 127

Writing Women: How I Do It - 129

The Counselor. Who Says Evil is Banal? - 133

Truckers, Earn While You Learn - 139

Thoughts that come in unbidden from the clouds
while mowing pasture and spoken
into a small recorder - 147

Ernest Thompson Seton, Malcolm X, and Me.
A Sort of Book Review. - 151

George Lois Made Me Do It - 159

What Is It About Montana Writers? - 169

Ioway Plates - 175

Leaving Billings - 181

Ski. If you can. All you can. - 187

Just for the Love of It - 193

I Always Wanted a Junkyard - 199

The Second Happiest Day: A Recommendation - 203

Rocky and the Rebel Punk - 209

Come Together. Right Now. - 219

COVID Days, Chocolate Nights - 225

Forget it, Jake. It's Hollywood. A Review. - 233

Make Me an Angel - 239

Lying for Fun and Profit - 245

To Live and Die in LA - 249

My Own Small Admissions Scandal - 261

Trinity - 265

Off Track—What I Did with One Hundred Dollars - 273

Acknowledgements - 283

AUTHOR'S NOTE

Kids are told lies all their young lives. If, when we grow up a little, we can unlearn some of the bullshit, we're better off, but not much. At eighty-three I've got a long way to go to get wisdom. As Jim Harrison said, (I'm paraphrasing here), I'm not sure I'm equipped to tell the truth. Some of the essays are memoiristic, some are just opinions. But, in remembering things, someone standing a few feet away and observing what I observed at ten years of age, or thirty, would most likely see it in a different way. So, I've tried to keep it all factual. Tony Schwartz, (not the Trump trumpeter, but the NY sound genius, who taught with Marshall McCluhan at Fordham University) interviewed and recorded a lot of New Yorkers; one of them said "That's my opinion and it's very true." I stand with that guy.

FOREWORD

WHEN I TURNED eighty (three years ago), my wife gave me a Fitbit Charge 2; a watch-like device I wear on my wrist and which tells me how many steps I've walked, my heart rate, things like that. The arbitrary goal seemed to be ten thousand steps in a day, as the watch buzzed and fireworks went off on its face when that occurred. So I've walked at least ten thousand steps a day since that birthday, and sometimes as many as fifteen thousand. I've passed fifteen million steps. They say it's about twenty million steps around the world. I was never a walker, though I worked out with weights and kept in pretty good shape, but then writing had me sitting a lot and a decline I associated with age set in. I urge you to get up and move around, Ms. Reader, Mr. Reader, whoever is kind enough to be holding this book. That's all, no preaching. Get up, move around, hydrate if you think of it. It's all good. (I upgraded to a Fitbit Charge 4 as I busted the crystal on the other one while doing chores. It still worked fine. Great piece of tech. The new one does everything but make me a sandwich.)

This good wife of mine also urged me to get two pups after a pair of beloved Australian Shepherds passed away within months of each other and brought me to my figurative knees. I didn't want to, but I'm so glad we got Cash and

Millie. The other day a man in a truck stopped, seeing me with the pups. He said, "Best dogs in the world. Wonderful companions." He watched them for a minute, drove on. I didn't know him, but I know something about him. I hope he gets some more dogs someday. He misses them.

Shortly after the old Aussies went, a horse we'd had for thirty years gave up and lay down, not to rise again. Just tired, he said. I was with him. Held his big head and talked to him. Then a good friend (who is chronicled in *The Horse Worrier*) passed away prematurely. I turned eighty and felt every bit of it. The two pups began to bring me around. The walking. The caring again. The writing. I searched my MacBook and located the nonfiction pieces I'd done over the last few years, starting with the horse piece that I wrote for an anthology some years ago, a CoCo Harris venture titled *Roll: A Collection of Personal Narratives*. A good book, if you think of it and would like a substantial book to read.

Lately I've been writing nonfiction pieces for literary reviews and various publications, and like the collections of poetry and short stories and novels I've done, I felt these might also be of interest to others. Some of the pieces are about writing, some are borne, like the wind carries weed seeds, of thoughts upon arising in the morning. Others are memoir.

Each morning I feed the two antic pups, the one remaining horse, a neighboring peacock that waits in the corral outside the buried electric fence that keeps the pups from chasing him off, and, in winter, as it is now, the wild birds. They feed on a downed mulberry tree that is still living and on a board affair I have rigged on the pasture fence. This operation takes about a half hour and puts about one thousand steps on my Fitbit. It also reaffirms that I'm here, in working order, and ready for another day. I don't know what could be better.

As Kurt Vonnegut said, "I urge you to please notice when you are happy, and exclaim or murmur or think at some point, 'If this isn't nice, I don't know what is."

Some stories are less than happy, for instance the one this book is named after. But that one needed to come out, to be shared. Some are downright silly, even if true (*Publishers Never Call*), and some are very hard to tell (*Racism by Default*) as they don't present me in the best light. Some are about the writing game, all are about the main game. Life. No particular order, no particular theme. They were all written by me, for me and you. The van Gogh piece was written for a book about that genius by a whole bunch of poets and authors, *Resurrection of a Sunflower*. Look it up. Big book, good book. You'll like it, especially if you like van Gogh, and who doesn't.

Chickens is the book between my last book of poetry and the next (*The Taste Of Red-Orange*). I didn't mean it to be; it just slid in there and demanded its place in line. So did another book of poetry titled *I Was in the Vicinity*. I was to be working on a thriller (*L.A. Hardscape*), but an upcoming sculpture show tricked me into writing *An Overdue Love Letter to Tensas Parish* because the sculpture is inspired by boyhood years there in St. Joseph, Louisiana. That, in turn, set me off on an essay-writing excursion, writing new ones, locating old ones, and here's the result. Some published, some not. I do hope it's as interesting for you to read as it surely was to write. It's a time machine for me. Some good trips and some not so, just as in the sixties. That essay has yet to be written, those sixties. Just for the record: I was never at Woodstock, though I can't remember for the life of me why not. If I write that one, it'll have to be fiction.

THE HORSE WORRIER

Horses haunt my life. They've owned me for more than half that hefty span. Being without them is not a reality to me. There have been at least fifty over the years, but about ten I remember vividly. I am not a trainer, nor am I, in any sense, an accomplished horseman. I have friends who are and, in this area, I'm sure they look down upon me in a rueful manner, shaking their wise heads.

There's an insert from one of these gents further along in this possibly ill-advised revelation, a man named Tim Trabon who braved broken collarbones, ribs, bruises that turned the color of beautiful Hawaiian postcards, and even malaria from his Amazon trips with Jacques Cousteau to get the better of these creatures. I digress. He gets his chance, as I said, later on when I defer to him and his haughty advice and tasteless jokes at my expense. This is *my* deal. He only gets a piece of it.

You'll immediately be aware of the difference in voice. He is true "horse people," and as such, insufferable. You'll see. Yet he is one of few "horse people" I will tolerate, being of good character otherwise.

I've had Quarter Horses (mainly), drafts, Appaloosas, grade horses, a Mexican Galiceno, Pasos, walking horses, Fox Trotters, Appendix-breds, and Saddlebreds, ponies in every color of the equine rainbow. Each one had a unique personality. Each one taught me something about life and about myself. Their teaching methods were varied but fell mainly into one of two camps: The "bad things happen fast" method and the "don't do that again" method. Often the two were combined. I've been kicked, bitten, rolled on, dragged, chased, bucked off, run off with, tree branched, and humiliated. I always came back for more.

I wanted one of those furry little Icelandic horses but found none available in Kansas. I had an outlaw paint Draft Horse shipped in from Nova Scotia by way of Kentucky, so anxious to be trampled am I. At great expense, I might add. Gentle giants, I was told. I was also told, in high school, that the cops couldn't chase you across the state line. I exploded both myths dramatically.

My relations with horses, as I've hinted, are not sound in the eyes of friends who are horse people. I once bought a Shetland pony (that should make me suspect to even the most rookie of horse fanciers), though I had a herd of eight or nine regular-sized horses. He was an agile little guy and could kick a large horse in the gut if pushed. He felt pushed often, being of cranky disposition. The other horses avoided him like rats are said to scram from sinking ships.

I bought him for my small children, but he didn't like them. He liked me. Mr. Walker was his name, and we had a game that possibly had its beginning after I'd had a few pops. I'd get on him, bareback. He'd buck me off over his head. I'd land on my feet. He'd wait patiently for me to get on him again. This could go on for a long time. I never reached his limit for this, but mine was about ten minutes. Then, as I was walking away, he'd thunder up behind me, slam on the brakes, and butt me with his head. I'd throw my arms out and pitch forward, running crazily, and he'd think that was fine. Once, he did that when it was muddy and he slid right over me. He actually seemed apologetic.

It's dangerous to anthropomorphize most animals, we are told, but we are also taught to do so by Disney movies and all the other Pixar propaganda poured into our souls from birth. At the Wise Compound, dogs talk and horses conspire. Toads live in mansions. It's a magical place where I slip back into childhood. Trabon warns of early dementia; these days, he says not so early after all. I've got a couple of years on him and, like most horse people, he snatches any perceived advantage greedily. Well, I may have fifteen years on him, but that doesn't make him young.

The horse obsession started early for me. I was way too young to know or care that horses attracted girls, but I became aware of this in high school and it added to my rationale. In fact, between marriages, it fueled the rationale.

I was a melodramatic child; I see this now as I look back. Nothing will distance you from parents and the world at large so much as stagecraft and idiocy packed into one. I rolled eyeballs back into foreheads like a laudanum overdose. I came by these histrionics historically, genetically. Much of the family had been artists, poets, politicians, opera-involved. Moody little French fur trapper forebears peered into campfires and saw their madness. One great uncle chased people about with his sword cane. Another did donuts on Missouri River ice in a 1938 Dodge automobile. All drank. Most were horse owners, some were ranchers. It was as though I was coached, little cheering sections of DNA hollering approval of over-the-top behavior. Denied a Daisy BB gun, I didn't mope. I quit eating. I held my breath. I penned my obituary. Eyeballs rolled.

When I was a kid in Tulsa, maybe nine, I cried myself into hiccup spasms under the back porch on weekend nights, with only Susie the gentle, old Springer Spaniel for company. She was my stepfather's duck dog. The reason for my inconsolable distress was, of course, that I desperately wanted a horse. This need went unrequited and unremarked. Even Susie slunk away.

I pleaded with my parents who, I see now, were somewhat sardonic anyway and had little patience for overwrought kids. My stepfather did one of his "I'll take care of this," hiking-up-his-pants moves, took me to a rancher acquaintance, and had him put me up on a high-powered cutting horse who dumped me early on, being used to knee signals that conflicted with whatever I was doing. A calf darted up out of a draw and I was airborne.

The long fall to the hard ground knocked the wind out of me and caused my old man to say, "Maybe we don't want a horsey after all, huh boy?" I sulled up and was quiet on the ride home, noting his smirk from time to time, having disposed of another annoying quirk from his inherited weird-acting kid.

No deal. I had been on a handsome creature and would climb aboard many more. It did happen eventually of course, just like an obsession with motorcycles panned out with dozens of those over my lifetime. I rodeoed as well, bull riding the event, never very good at it until too old, then pulled-off ligaments in my right arm hit me like a gunshot, and off I went from a bull I was actually winning on in a California rodeo. The Tulsa cutting horse incident was merely a small part of the trailer for the movie. The obsession lay in wait like chickenpox is said to reside in your spinal base until released years later. Like Trabon's malaria knocks him for a loop every ten years or so.

My first real love, my high-school sweetheart, had a horse. Was that the reason we were so entwined? I don't think so; no, I *know* that's not the reason. She was a green-eyed, raven-haired beauty. It was a combination of chemicals, physical attraction, and that collision of pheromones that afflicts teens, plus something indefinable but unmistakable that people call love. With all this going on, it's a miracle that I even graduated. Her horse, Midnight, a rangy, ribby character, was stabled at a Kansas City establishment that still exists, Benjamin Stables. We rode together on the picturesque trails there. I participated in their rodeos sometime later, after this girl and I had taken vastly different forks in the road.

In college I found time, between classes and working at Miller's 66 gas station, to locate a riding/boarding stable. This was at Westminster, in Fulton, Missouri. There I found a friend named Buck, a compact buckskin horse, who seemed to welcome my visits. He belonged to a fellow who appeared to be a good owner and who allowed me to ride Buck occasionally and to bring him an apple or two. I learned a little about treats and dietary functions from this man. "Don't ever give him an apple unless I'm here and say it's okay," he told me. "He might have just had some grain, and that apple would ferment in his gut and colic him up." Colic, it was explained to me, was a killer. Unfortunately, I was to see it more than once years later in its most evil intestine-wracking form. I will say that happenstance caused it, not carelessness or ignorance on my part.

At any rate, I married a horsewoman while still in college, and it wasn't long before we'd found a way to own horses, both of us possessing a similar indifference to facts and life lessons. Like a lot of young horsey fools, we felt that, with enough horses, we could make money on them. Start a business! Board and train! Buy and sell!

If I were a banker and an earnest couple with similar intentions came to me with such a plan, I'd laugh them out the front door. In a hurry. And don't come back! I have never seen a horse operation succeed. Other than those big-money racing stables, and I suspect they cover up negative cash flow hemorrhages with infusions from various trusts and foundations as Byzantine as the casino business.

I won't delve further into the business aspects of horses; no reason to—I'll just say there *are* no business aspects and leave it at that. Here's an ad for a horse that completely captivated Tim Trabon. He bought the horse. The horse proved untenable. In spades. He gave the horse to a Mexican trainer who says, to this day, "Best horse I ever had." The horse was a pure and vicious outlaw here in the Midwest. Some legendary horsemen had a go with him. One such cowboy got bucked off three times in a few minutes. This is not to say Mexican trainers are any better, just that a "go figure" attitude goes a long way in the horse "business." Plus, Tim suspects that the horse is really a pile of bones in the Sonoran Desert and his Mexican friend is, like most horse people, into saving face big time.

TS Winning Dust Bar
1998 15.1 hand Bay Gelding AQHA #3669348
The best broke, gentlest gelding money can buy

(John & Jane Doe) are bringing us one of their best home-raised geldings with this cute, Shapey gelding. "Scooter" has been raised the right way right from the very start, so he's never learned any bad habits. When (John & Jane) say a horse is broke, you can take it to the bank because it will do just about everything but make you coffee. Scooter can handle any job you give him whether it's win a buckle in working cow-horse classes or pack the kitchen sink to the top of the mountain. If you're looking for a horse that will shine in the arena for working ranch horse, reined cow horse, ranch cutting, heeling, pleasure or dressage Scooter will do you proud. He has carried packs and riders over every type of rough country and brought everything and everyone back in one piece. Scooter can execute flying lead changes, spins, sliding stops, cut, pen and rope a cow, jump, and do cantering pirouettes. He's been exposed to every spooky thing imaginable and lived to tell about it. Scooter will lay down on command and get in your back pocket. He stays broke between rides and loves people and attention. These are the kind that everyone wants but only come along occasionally. (John & Jane) are offering one week of free lessons with Scooter to the lucky person that gets him at their school in (No Name), MT. Video available

SOLD Congratulations Tim Trabon Buyer

Quite an animal, wouldn't you say? Now these people probably stretched the truth only a little. They are of good repute. Something may have happened in the walnut-sized brain of this horse to turn him south. Or he may have had a pain problem of some kind that later dissipated. Or, as Tim says, this seller is a top hand, and a rank animal might be a fine ride as far as he's concerned. I'm only saying never ever buy a horse from an ad or online unless you can go to the source and spend weeks riding it.

Roxy came to me from the evil ethers, the internet. A friend in Albuquerque found her and sent me her picture. I should mention this friend owns mustangs, so she enjoys a challenge. She has ground-trained these horses from wild blurs of now you see them, now you don't, to accepting a halter in mid-pasture. If you think this isn't some kind of accomplishment I heartily recommend giving it a shot. The picture she sent was of a gorgeous paint draft filly running. My thought was that I could use this magnificent animal for sculpture reference, having made a couple of life-sized drafts out of welded steel before. I just didn't know it would require exorcism.

Her original name was Paris of Avalon. Forms a picture right there, does it not? She was a beautiful filly, fifty-percent Clydesdale, and I anticipated she'd be gentle as a spring zephyr. I should have taken more notice when she was unloaded at Wise Acres as a young filly. She seemed to lean on and pull the driver as he brought her to me. He said, "She only does that because she's a little insecure; it doesn't mean she's trying to control or anything." I put her in with Harley and Lopez, the two horses I had left from my many adventures over the years. Lopez promptly ran her into a fence and cut her up. I cleaned and treated the wounds, surprised at Lopez's vicious attack. He was getting old and possibly felt he had to establish his place in the herd as soon as he could. She kept out of his way until she gained some size, and that happened quickly. Then she was merciless in her revenge. She also knocked *me* butt over tea kettle just for the hell of it, a rotator-cuff injury reminding me of her playfulness with the added advantage of forecasting rain. She often squealed when thwarted, the classic fight sound of a horse at the edge of her stress envelope. Trabon helped me with her, as you'll see.

But there was one horse out of all the others that was magic. He spoiled me for all time, made me think that I was some kind of natural horseman, pumped my ego way up, and became, in a very short time, my partner. His name was Thor when I first laid eyes on him. God of war. And he did look somewhat like a war horse. Roman nose, roched mane, ass end like a boxcar, muscled front, feathered hooves. Thor was a buckskin who came to Iowa from Arizona and had been a hazing horse, from what sketchy information anyone could pass along about him. He was maybe twelve, a grade horse with some Percheron to him—big, husky, built like an oversized Foundation Quarter Horse. He was beautiful. I first saw him as a head jutting out of a barn window hole. He looked like a Frazetta comic book horse—something Death Dealer might ride into a horde of Mongols as he finished them off.

I had been advised that Thor was for sale, the price being $250. I committed to him without seeing any of the rest of him. That magnificent head was it for me. Fortunately, the rest of him was commensurate. I approached the barn and talked to him; in turn, I was approached by his owner. What followed was one of the weirdest horse-oriented conversations I've ever experienced.

"You want something?" Not a welcoming tone.

"Yeah, this horse is for sale I understand?"

"To the killers. I'm sellin' him for dog meat."

"Uh, why would that be?"

"Sumbitch drug me on a gravel road."

"How much the killers paying for him?"

"Don't care. They can have him for free."

Back in those days the renderers paid one hundred dollars or more for a horse. Now, you have to pay them.

"But I'll pay more than they will."

"Don't care. Want him dead."

This person had been drinking fairly heavily, and it was only about 10 am on a Saturday morning. At that time of my life I was a drinker, but like a lot of lushes, didn't start until noon. That way, I felt I had control over it. I didn't, of course, but it's beside the point. I'd heard this guy was a knee-walking, snot-flying lush and that he mistreated this horse and various other animals. He'd lost his license and now used Thor as transportation to a downtown bar, where he tied him in the alley until such time as he rolled out of the bar and rode him home. Apparently, on one of these homecomings, Thor's owner had slipped sideways and been dragged along, probably at a walk judging from the fact he was still with us.

I changed the subject and we had more of a normal conversation, and then I acted like I was about to leave.

"Nice meeting you, Tom," I said. "It was a pleasure." Nothing could be farther from the truth. This guy was a boor and a pissant.

"Yeah. Stop by for a beer sometime." He gestured at the barn. Maybe he lived there.

"Sure will," I said.

"Hell, have one now." He ducked into the barn and returned with two wet cans fresh from an ice-filled cooler, popped one, and gave me the other.

We drank, smoked, talked about the difficulties of living one's own life without being jacked around by various authorities and bluenoses. Then the subject of Thor came up.

"You want that horse?"

"Yes, I'd like to have him all right."

He appeared to be on the verge of sullenness again, thought for a moment, and said, "You can have him if you take him right now."

"Do you have a saddle and bridle I can borrow?"

"I don't loan out tack. Do I look like a fucking moron?"

Yes, you do! I wanted to answer. *And butt ugly, too.*

"Well, how can I take him right now?"

"That's your problem. I need $250 cash money."

Fortunately I'd brought just that and handed it over. He counted it twice. Meantime, I searched around the outside of the barn and came up with some baling twine and a green piece of branch that I cut with a pocketknife. I had never tried this before, but I fashioned a bit out of the stick and attached the twine to both ends, and then tied another piece of twine around the rig and Thor's nose to stabilize it after I'd fitted the bit in his mouth. I led him to a good-sized rock and hoisted myself up on his back, fully expecting him to cut loose on me once I got aboard. Nothing. He stood quietly. Even Tom seemed taken aback. He had opened another beer without offering me one and sat with his back against the barn, scowling as though he'd been taken advantage of.

"I'll be back for my car," I said.

Without waiting for an answer, I wheeled Thor around and to the tractor path that led to the gravel road. I gave him a little touch in the ribs with my heels, and he jigged up to a fast trot which I slowed to a walk. I had maybe two miles to go with a major highway to cross on the journey. There was no drama on the trip. It was as though the horse and I had been a duo forever. I renamed him Percy on the way to celebrate his obvious Percheron heritage, and I talked to him constantly. We had to use the median of the highway for a quarter-mile, and the passing trucks and cars didn't seem to bother him beyond a naturally intelligent wariness.

When we rode through a residential area, dogs didn't spook him, but I felt him bunch up a little if one got close, preparing to kick if he needed to.

We finally arrived at his new home, Porky Dexter's pig farm, where a group of us had rented a house and a barn and installed a personable young man to oversee it. We called the place Lazy Frank's Dirt Farm. Percy took to it. I put him in a holding pen and watched him while I waited for someone to show up and take me to my car. That was the start of an amazing sixteen-year relationship, one that made me think all horses were very special animals. Many weren't. Percy was. I mentioned I was a drinker back then. Percy didn't like Tom, his former owner, and I thought that dislike and mistrust would ignite if I ever approached Percy with a snootful. The very smell of alcohol would mask the fact that I had good intentions. I needn't have worried. He did everything he could to stay underneath me.

Nobody else could ride Percy. Lazy Frank tried and gave up. Percy didn't like women, we discovered. He'd back through a three-rail fence with a female rider on his back. He only acted normal with me on him. I say normal; he had his predilections. A man in a metallic-green Pontiac slowed down on the road while I was on Percy to ask me directions. He rolled down his window on the passenger side and started to ask—Percy turned his butt broadside to the car and kicked his door in. The Pontiac threw gravel getting out of there and I didn't see it again.

Once, a police car stopped us at about 3 am, and the driver informed me that in that Iowa county any moving conveyance was required to have a red light to the rear. "Shoot, did that thing go out again?" I said, and they, too, threw gravel, laughing upon departure. Percy was bunched and ready to do damage to the vehicle, but I held him in. Blitzed as I was, I knew better than to vandalize public property.

The spirits (Jack Daniels and a host of night shapes) moved me to ride late at night. It felt like freedom. Percy and I would range here and there, through pastures, over hills and an American Indian burial mound, or so we would conjecture, gathering up what spirits awaited in the inky night, canter down roads we knew, and discover byways. I would sing at the top of my voice; usually, the song was "Hooley-ann" and I would put Percy's name in place of "Old Paint." Whenever his name came up, his ears would stand at attention.

"I ride an ol' Percy, I lead an ol' Dan, I'm goin' to Montana to throw the Hooley-ann. Ol' Bill Jones had a daughter and a son, son went college and the daughter went wrong, wife got killed in a poolroom fight and still he keeps singin' from mornin' to night." And we would ride into the night, sleep, and the day job be damned.

My own gravel-road situation came up on one of these rides. Percy, like a lot of horses, bloated a bit when you'd cinch him up, thereby loosening the cinch strap afterward, for comfort's sake. Usually I would compensate for this by cinching it a hair tighter. Not this time. I dimly recall hoisting myself up onto him and falling off the other side. He stood quietly, craning his neck to watch this spectacle. Finally, I was aboard and we began another night adventure.

I must have "fallen asleep," as we say in the program, and something went haywire. It was a gravel road, and I was, shoulder to gravel, upside down, my feet caught in the stirrups—the saddle had slipped underneath his belly. I said "whoa," and Percy stopped. Perhaps he had already stopped. This situation would have been perilous on any other horse in the universe. He watched with a gracefully curved neck while I worked at getting one foot out, then the other. I had ahold of one rein and lost that in the process. I fell beneath him with a thump, watching his four legs. I stood shakily, gathered the reins, leaned against his warm shoulder, and thanked him over and over. I righted the saddle, cinched it snugly, and we rode back home. I have never forgotten that incident, testimony to friendship and the patience of a horse who had little patience for other horses, people, automobiles, or blowing leaves. Yet, he stood for me. He put up with me. What streamed through my mind as I hung below him, was how Tom, the other lush, had been dragged on a gravel road. Was I to suffer the same fate? I deserved it, no doubt in my mind. I even accepted it to a degree. Thank god and Percy for mercy. A hoof in the head would have ended things right then and there.

Percy hated (yes, hated) to be passed by another horse. This was evident when the gang from Lazy Frank's got together and rode on beautiful fall days, all of us feeling like The Hole in the Wall Bunch, hoorawing and riding over flatland prairie, down the roads and through the draws. He would stretch out his handsome head, ears pasted to his skull, and I could feel the effort as he would keep distance between us and other riders. I should have taken this into consideration when, on a daft whim, I entered him in a western pleasure class at a horse show. We took the kids to horse shows back then, and they did well in various classes. I sometimes took Percy to these events to ride him around the perimeters of the fairgrounds and to let him partake of the noises and excitement of the shows; he enjoyed going and we had fun being together.

Picture a horse that cannot *stand* to be passed by another horse, in an oval arena full of other horses, which, at some point, *have* to pass him. We are all in there, moving counterclockwise, being told to walk, trot, and then canter. It was during the latter command that Percy decided *To hell with this, I'm passing everything in the ring*. And he did.

Several times. *Hang on,* he telegraphed to me, *I'm hauling ass and taking names.* I was over his neck like a jockey coming up on a camera finish. He was throwing dirt clods into the crowd, and I heard shouts of glee; the race was on. But it was an unwinnable race because there were always more horses to pass. Finally, the judges called for us to bring our horses into the center and stand. Percy was lathered and antsy, so I backed him, which often brought him back to calm—in so doing I backed into a judge and was told to leave the arena. They opened the gate and we left. I was bathed in shame, but Percy left in a jaunty trot and a bit of a side pass to show what fun he'd had. I told him he'd done well, patted his shoulder, dismounted, and walked him until he had cooled off. He seemed pleased.

In the next fifteen years, we moved from Iowa to Wisconsin, then back to Kansas, and Percy was always there. In Wisconsin, we had a neighbor with a green tennis court, and he called from time to time to say Percy was on it. It was a hard court, so we never learned what his attachment to it was; he just liked standing on it. Across the road was the Milwaukee Country Club, and Percy and his good friend Señor would sometimes join the golfers, who played through the grazing duo. Fences were toughened and horses (and greenskeepers) were kept in abeyance.

During one of our moves, we had to pasture Percy with some other horses until we could bring him to our own place. The owner called me and tried to explain what Percy was doing; finally, I drove out there to see what he was talking about. The other horses, a herd of maybe twelve, were all bunched together by a corner of fence. Percy was grazing maybe fifty feet away from them. When one would decide to squirt out one side, Percy would just lay his ears back and that horse would return to the group immediately.

The owner said, "So you see why he can't stay. He'll starve the rest of them, being some kind of pasture boss."

I made arrangements to bring him to the place sooner than later. He knew our horses and would allow them to graze. Now and then.

Sixteen years with an antic a day is a lot of material. This horse was one in a million. I may have to jot those antics all down so I'll have them if memory starts to fail, but for now, he remains fresh in my mind and I see him now and then, in my buckskin Harley, when dusk announces night. Harley is nothing like Percy except in color, but when he gazes off toward the cows in the next pasture, I see something that reminds me of him.

Ernest Thompson Seton said, "the life of a wild animal always has a tragic end," and so it was with Percy, as he began to lose his sight and invulnerability. But he taught me things. And he showed me things about myself that I shied away from and later managed to confront. Who knows, maybe his dignity will show up in me someday.

Too somber a note for such a wonderful personality. I won't end on that because it's just not Percy. Anyway, we figure his life span was in the thirties and he certainly showed unmistakable signs of enjoying most of it hugely.

Back to Trabon. Horse people.

I have one of Tim's horses; an ex-athlete named Mighty Mouse. Mighty replaced Paris of Avalon and Roxy, who wanted to maim me. She moved on to a lover of draft horses who trained her nicely and loves her dearly. He has a beautiful place and his son is a vet. She hit the horsey jackpot. I lost a ton of stress.

My one other horse, a high-strung Appendix-bred buckskin has been with me since shortly after his birth twenty-two years ago. My wife, Freddie, bought him for me, and we separated him from his mother on our place. He held a grudge for some time, but we've finally come to a friendship of sorts. He spent a summer as a cow horse and when he returned he was a rideable sort who would still spook at a blowing piece of paper. As Sean, the cowboy who rode him sunup to sundown, said, "He tends to spazz out when he sees ... well, anything." But he was one-hundred percent better than when he would buck me off time and again. I could feel it coming now, and that was an improvement.

And my Mexican horse was the smoothest ride I'd ever encountered, a Cadillac in any gait. He passed away on the place after many years and is buried here. But that would leave Harley alone, and a herd animal longs for the company of his own kind. Hence, phasing in Roxy the killer draft horse as Lopez aged. He liked her a lot, but I didn't. So, Trabon arranged a trade for which I am grateful. He found Roxy a super home. And he brought me Mighty Mouse. The hardcore cowboys who run his ranch had wanted to put MM down as he was lame and not of working use anymore. Tim said no, emphatically. MM had been a marvelous cutting horse and ranch-using horse for a good while, and he was only about fourteen.

The day they took Roxy, Harley was beside himself. He trotted all over the pasture hollering for her. But Tim had arranged for a near-seamless trade, and MM was in my holding pen. I turned him out and hoped for the best, which did happen. Harley looked him over—they sniffed around on one another—and relaxed into an easy grazing partnership. Nary a squeal was ever heard, no fighting stance.

Mighty is very Western. He thinks I'm a sap, that's obvious. But I feed him a special supplement called RecoveryEQ and he is showing signs of getting better, even running now and then, which Harley likes to do. The two horses are quite happy. They are asked to do little other than stand for their twice-yearly shots and get their hoofs trimmed every few months. They submit to this without any fuss, and I watch them, using them for reference for my sculpture of life-sized steel horses. Quid pro quo. Plus, I get to see them, period. A true pleasure. The farrier, Terry Holmes, calls them pasture ornaments and voices his criticisms of me by talking to the horses. "Stop that, you fat sumbitch. Maybe somebody'd ride you now and then, you'd lose some weight." Terry is horse people.

Sometimes, they lurk far off in the pasture and I holler for them to come up for their small amount of feed. I like to check them over for wounds of any kind, see how they are moving. One time, they refused to come. I got down on one knee and this provoked them to move closer, ears up, furrowed brows. Then they stopped. So I lay down and flopped an arm now and then. They trotted closer, blowing and snorting. I flopped some more. They moved closer. It's a technique I developed which I call "horse-worrying." It works when you need to get their attention *in pasture* as they say. Which is a little like *in country* or *in situ*. I got it from the movie *The Horse Whisperer*, from the scene where Redford hunkers down in situ to watch a recalcitrant horse for, who knows, hours, until said horse finally gets it and approaches him to do all his bidding.

I shared this bit of horsemanship with Trabon, and here is his answer via email:

> *My prescribed method for haltering a horse involves me throwing the rope end of the halter over their necks. Once that's done, they know they're caught and start hunting the halter with their nose. Maybe you do it that way, I don't know. I'm beginning to suspect that you might pantomime putting the halter on yourself*

in an attempt to allay their fears as well as gain their favor. That way would probably take a bit more time than my method.

I haven't tried the rolling-around-on-the-ground bit. I just whistle every time I feed them and they associate my whistling with "probably should head towards the barn; food."

Before I taught myself to whistle, I just rang a bell. At the Haythorn they have an old time siren off an ambulance or something. They wind that baby up and you better get out of the way because a shit load of horses are coming.

I bought a yearling, actually I bought 3 of them, this time two years ago. My friend Jim agreed to take care of them, and for doing so, I let him take his pick.

He chose a rangy-looking bay with long legs and alert eyes. That left a chestnut horse and a red roan. When they turned two, I took them to [A name I will delete here. I, too, have had difficulties with this person. – author note] with the intent he might start them for me.

Being a true cowboy, he preferred to forget about that and instead get married, get drunk, get divorced, and then run away and get drunk again.

So I picked up my two untouched horses and took them to another trainer who lives south of you.

The red roan is an outlaw who will fool you into thinking he's gentle, and then buck you off and try to kick you as you sail through the air.

The chestnut, at this point, may end up being the finest horse I may ever own.

The whole point of me setting up this story is so that I might tell you about riding him last night.

I was at the Saddle and Sirloin Club riding him in an arena. He's only three years old and has maybe twenty-five rides on him, all of them within the confines of an arena.

A friend of mine rode up and asked me to ride with him across the club's 300 acres so that he could inspect some erosion.

I declined, stating the few rides this horse had had and the fact that the temperature was dropping and blustery wind usually bothered any horse I ever rode. I also had not yet taught this horse how to stop. He said he understood and rode off.

I sat a moment and thought that I was going to have to buck up and ride him out at some point, and I might as well get it over with.

Trying to suppress the anxiety rising up within me, I trotted out of the arena and caught up with my friend

My little horse looked around quizzically as we crossed ditches, rode through heavy timber, and spooked a couple of deer. He acted as if all of this was no big deal. I was astonished. Any other horse I ever rode out for the first time either spooked and ran off a little or bucked me off and left me lying on the ground.

I haven't come up with a name for this horse yet but I am going to ask Patti if she'll let me bring him in the house any time it gets too cold outside. He's a solid citizen at the tender age of three, and at this point, there just isn't anything too good for him.

So, you see, Tim and I do share some attributes, though he is, by far, the better horseman. I have never seen anyone work at it harder, and his effort pays off with more abilities learned and techniques mastered.

But he has also taken on some of the coloration of "horse people" and that's, well, sad. They're control freaks who sashay around horse events with derogatory comments at the ready.

I could go on and on with crazy stuff my horses have done over the years and crazier stuff I have done, but as another horse fancier of the pari-mutuel persuasion (my uncle, Reno Pete, lifelong gambler and bettor) used to say, "Screw 'em all but eight; six to carry you and two to pull the wagon." In my case, one of those two would surely be Percy. But even in traces, he would always be ahead of the other one.

KNUCKLEHEAD

MAYBE I INHALED too much model airplane fuel when I was building those free-flight gasoline-powered planes as a kid. I know I loved the smell of garages and anything that ran on any kind of fuel at all. I got to mow lawns in the fifties with a rope-start power mower that belonged to a neighbor—I got paid, but I'd eagerly have done it for free. I internalized internal combustion. Those little airplane engines went from stone dead to snarling angry life with the help of a battery and a finger placed just right on the prop, then flipped. You learned early how to do that after the propeller chewed up your index finger. There was danger involved with all of this stuff. Adrenaline. Proximity of combustibles. Heat. Heady vapors. A greasy blue cloud world of its own, and I loved it.

So, 1953. Before Elvis. Saturday. We were hanging out, bored. Levi's, T-shirts, hoodlumesque enough to get a peek from a neighbor's window, the curtain falling back into place as we looked. I was barely fifteen.

"Let's go to a show," said Maury. He knew all the movies, what was showing. "*The Wild One* is on at the Plaza. It's about gangs. Motorcycles. They take over this little town." Motorcycles. Yikes. I had always wanted one. I rented BSAs with a driver's license not my own. I borrowed a

Cushman Eagle from an older friend who was outgrowing it. I borrowed a Zündapp from a rich kid who didn't care about it. I borrowed a lowly Solex from another friend—it was a bicycle that you pedaled up to speed, and then lowered a little kerosene-powered motor on a hinge down on the front wheel, which would keep you going for an hour. Pretty dorky, but it had a motor. I had lots of miles on bikes with playing-card-spoke motors, and then motor-propelled scooters and motorcycles. And here was a movie about people on such conveyances exercising undreamed-of powers. A true must-see.

We saw it. My god. I can remember parts of it to this day. I absorbed it like model airplane glow fuel, inhaled it, lived it. When that waitress asked Brando what he was rebelling against, and he said "'Whaddya got?'" it caused me to wait, in vain, for years for someone to ask me that, so I could answer, in a barely intelligible mumble, "'Whaddya got?'" The question never came.

An aside: never see a movie over again later in life that affected you deeply. Just don't. If you have, you know what I mean. See it in your head, and it will retain its power. See it on the screen, many years later, and it's WTF? This movie was, is, an embarrassment. It's, well, stupid. Poorly directed. Sucky dialogue. Just dopey. Most of them didn't even ride Harleys, . What did I know? I wanted a Velocette that I'd seen in *Popular Mechanics*. A *French* motorcycle! With a shaft drive! *Zut alors!*

But it wasn't dopey in 1953. It was revelatory. It was a religious experience.

I emerged, slit-eyed, into the sunlight, barely listening to my friends. It was a new world. I was changed. Within days I would own my first Harley-Davidson. I would wear motorcycle boots. I aspired to take over a small town with a newly-acquired band of friends, nascent criminals, and mentally unbalanced pals. We would mumble like Brando. Roll our eyes. Smirk.

I had a small stash of paper-route money that I had saved up due to my mom often declaring we were bankrupt. She used that term whenever something like a new car or a move was out of reach. Then she'd paint the living room.

So, instead of saving the family, I made a down payment on a well-worn Harley-Davidson Knucklehead. The nickname derives from the fact that the rocker boxes atop the finned cylinder heads resembled two knuckles of a fist. I negotiated for five-dollar–a-week payments on this monster. The older kid I bought it from fired it up for me and that whole gasoline/olfactory thing kicked in—plus the unmistakable sound effects of that big, chunky Harley-falling-apart sound. I was in heaven. I never knew the year of this hog, just the aura. It had a tank shift and a scary clutch which was later to be my downfall. I'm embarrassed to say I don't know if it was a sixty-one cubic inch or a seventy-four. I'll say seventy-four because that's preferred these days. I was never *not* scared on this thing. And always delighted.

One small problem. Well, about six small problems. I didn't have a driver's license. There was no way I could title the thing, so I had no license plate. And my folks were dead set against motorcycles. A big NO. End of discussion. So I bypassed them, kept it at Ray C.'s house, a two-block walk from my own. My paper route got me up at 5 a.m.—after throwing the route from Mr. Ehlers' paper truck (I had the right side and a left-handed kid took the other. We could lead a dog with these flat-sailing *Kansas City Times* and bounce one right off his head. We were good), I had free time until school and it was still dark at that time of year. I'd coast down Ray's driveway and jump-start the Knucklehead halfway down the block. And I'd cruise Brookside and all around Midtown, the wind in my face, the Harley thrumming a deep, dirty sound bubble all around me. Dark, chilly freedom. Citizens slept unaware of the grinning, budding menace in goggles invading their streets.

I don't think any non-biker can know the ... theosophy of this. The Zen. Maybe a surfer would know. A skier alone on an expert run with that once-in-a-season rhythm on the moguls. Yeah, there are parallels. But, in the main, it's like the T-shirt says: "It's a Harley thing. You wouldn't understand." I don't think the graying, paunchy baby boomers, the Rolex Riders, understand, but I could be wrong.

I was fifteen. Elvis and James Dean and *Catcher in the Rye* would help mold my persona a bit later. For now I was putty in the hands of William Harley and Walter Davidson.

Later in my life, I would move my family to Milwaukee for the chance to work on Harley-Davidson advertising. To this day I own a Harley. There is no antidote.

I digress. There was, as I said, no license plate on the knucklehead. Fortuitously, at that time, Wheaties cereal packaged small license plates in their boxes for a premium. These plates were embossed metal and about the size of a motorcycle plate. Missouri motorcycle plates were white with black letters back then, and the only ones that Wheaties offered in that color combination were Maine, Quebec, British Columbia, and a couple of other oddball plates. My memory tells me I got Alaska, even though it wasn't a state until 1959, but I'll go with that. I hung it on the back of the tractor-type saddle with hanger wire. I was never stopped. My folks were a bit puzzled at my accelerated appetite for Wheaties (until the plate showed up), but dismissed it; "He's a growing boy."

Memory. This is the strange part; I can't even remember the Knucklehead's color, although I think it may have been red. I'm pretty sure it was. What I recall in detail is the total and complete emancipation from the humdrum, the routine. The liftoff. I had no loyalty to brand or configuration or fine points back then. I was in it for the fix, the release. The Harley loyalty came later, and it was always tied to my first, albeit brief, ownership experience.

A few weeks and about thirty bucks more of payments into this adventure, Maury and I took the Knucklehead over to Loose Park with a stopwatch. Loose Park had a paved sidewalk all around it in 1953, and we used it for lap timing runs. He'd clock me and vice versa, and we'd try to beat one another's times. That day, under a cloudless, sparkling blue sky, on my third or fourth attempt, I decided to wind out low gear much faster and pop it into second, to get up to speed early. The clutch was referred to as a beartrap, and it wasn't made for such shenanigans. Something sickening happened. I missed the shift, the bike lurched as though I'd hit the brakes, and the sound of gear parts and transmission crunches were evident. Then it freewheeled. We walked it home.

Later that week, I called the kid I'd bought it from. Said my folks wouldn't let me keep it and something was broken in the transmission anyway. He said no refunds; I agreed. And he came and picked it up in a panel truck.

But I was hooked. And beginning to figure out that Harleys had magical properties built into them at the factory, probably with incantations and ceremonies. I wasn't far off.

I visited the factory back in the sixties, having moved to Milwaukee and signed on to Harley-Davidson's advertising agency. I'll never forget two things about that visit. The first was: Walter Davidson, son or maybe grandson to the original Davidson, despised any changes to Harley-Davidson factories so he made all the chopper owners park their machines outside the chain-link fence to the parking lot. This effectively advertised the choppers and called attention to their modifications and bizarre designs, propagating more of the same.

The other thing that imprinted on me was what I call "The Skronk Effect." On the tour, I was led past a bearded and tattooed worker with a chain-drive pocketbook and a weathered leather jacket. He would affix a two-sided flywheel counterweight in a vise, then take a two-by-four, insert it in between the two pieces of iron, and force the pieces apart with a noise that sounded like "skronk." Then he would un-vise it and toss it atop a growing pile of these things.

I asked my guide about this operation and he said, "Well, ol' Ernie is adjusting counterweights so they don't wobble and shake the bike too much." My next question was, "Are they adjusted further somewhere down the line?"

"Naw. Ernie's got a purty good feel for this."

I only vaguely recall their museum. In my memory it was a big, dark unheated room with broken factory windows and old motorcycles parked along the walls. Then, above these, was a shelf-like rack where more were jammed in together. I believe there was one for each year since their inception, but it was such an agglomeration of frames, pipes, and motors that the initial visual effect was that of a parking lot at a biker bar at night.

Easy Rider came out that year, and outlaw bikes took on longer front forks and higher handlebars than ever before. I had bought a Harley-Davidson police bike from Precinct Five in Milwaukee at about the same time. The main bearings were fried and it was otherwise in disrepair. I hauled it home and began tearing it down, but I borrowed so many tools from my mechanic neighbor that he wordlessly wheeled the hulk over to his barn and that's where it was transformed.

I took the v-twin motor to the factory where it was rebuilt and bored out. I had admired the front tube forks of Peter Fonda's Harley in *Easy Rider* (they were eight inches over stock length) so I ordered a pair from Cheetah Motorcycle Parts in California. I waited for that box with the same anticipation and impatience that, in boyhood, I'd exhibited while awaiting a Lone Ranger Atom Bomb ring (really, there was such a thing, though it makes no sense whatsoever) from Battle Creek, Michigan.

There had been a mistake and these were not eight inch over stock length; they were eighteen inch over stock length! We re-raked the gooseneck on the frame, and installed them. I was on the way to owning a chopper that would never be allowed within miles of the Harley-Davidson plant. No front fender. Curlicue handlebars. Camel hump seat. Bored-out "eighty over."

The tank: we cut the fat bob double tank in half lengthways, so it had the same profile from the side, but looking down at it, it was long and skinny. It was a tank shift motorcycle with first, second, third ... and reverse! It had been set up for use with a sidecar for some reason that was never satisfactorily explained to me, but the reverse now came in handy. With the super-long fork, it was a bear to turn around in tight spaces, but a reverse gear would make it more manageable.

My mechanic friend declared it unsafe at any speed or standing still, wiped his hands, and turned to more conservative endeavors. Like installing a huge hemi engine in a small hatchback, mid-engine so the driver was inches from it.

This perversion of the Harley-Davidson ideals would have had a longer story, but economic realities cut it short. The deep well pump failed at the house we had bought on the rural outskirts of Milwaukee, and the first item up for sale was this chopper. My wife and kids weren't going to give up showers. A member of the Milwaukee Outlaws club bought it, paid cash in hundred dollar bills, slapping them down on my kitchen table. The motorcycle was unfinished, frame apart from engine, but savvy eyes could surely see the possibilities. I like to think it is bellowing somewhere on the Wisconsin streets and highways, emitting menace, exacting awe.

It would have narrowed the eyes of the older Mr. Davidson to Clint Eastwood gun turrets. I think Willie G. Davidson, a progressive sort, and designer of the wildly successful machines to come after the buyback from AMF, might have grinned. He might have withheld enthusiastic approval, however, just on the basis of engineering principles, if not aesthetics.

I have owned Harleys since then. And Triumphs, and BSAs, and a BMW. But Harleys have been the stalwarts over the years. I still own one. Chopped, raked, lowered. It sits in back of a 1949 Ford in the metal building where I weld steel sculptures. It's a beauty. But it's no Knucklehead.

A drug addict once told me that his whole life until rehab had been an unrelenting search for the euphoria of his first original high. I know my first cup of Kona coffee in the morning on a Saturday is the best. The subsequent cups are really good, don't get me wrong, but the first sip of the first cup is nirvana. And, sometimes, as I'm sipping that, I'm looking at email or the Saturday paper and wasting that effect on some level. Like the knucklehead I surely am after all these years.

I didn't have any such sidebars or distractions when I first straddled that Harley. I was into it. I twisted that throttle and the sound went from the distinctive "potato, potato" idle to a ragged elk holler. It went through me. I *was* that sound. I *was* that knucklehead. Like the T-shirt says, "It's a Harley thing. You wouldn't understand." I'm not sure I do either.

THE UNNATURALIST

I CAN REMEMBER the moment I stopped hunting forever. I was outside Omaha, great pheasant country then, in the sixties. I'd gone out alone, a friend having bailed due to another obligation, and though I'd miss the company, I did like the fields and the woods on a fall day when winter was clearly setting in. There was an edge to the cold and a gray, forbidding sky.

I still smoked back then, and I was in a small clearing by a deserted farmhouse; I laid my shotgun in a solid spot, fished out my cigarette pack, shook one out, and lit it. It was the clink of the Zippo that spooked them out. Pheasants were everywhere, it seemed. As I recounted it later, there must have been fifty of them, and I see no reason to modify that figure, unbelievable as it seems, especially today.

I was transfixed, cigarette in one hand, lighter in the other, mouth undoubtedly open. The noise was like several clotheslines of wash in a fierce wind, and suddenly over. The birds, iridescent necks of blues and greens, flashed by, out of the weeds and brush in the farmyard, and I was struck by the beauty of them. And the question occurred: why shoot them? Followed by others: what's it prove? I know I can. But, man, they are beauties.

I sat on a log, opened my thermos of coffee, and poured in a splash of bourbon, something I did usually after hunting was done.

And hunting *was* done. Was it ever. I drank and smoked and marveled at what I'd seen, and a few small snowflakes drifted into the farmyard.

By the time I'd finished the coffee toddy, the snowflakes were larger and I began to think of home and the fireplace, the latter unused since the year before. I hadn't fired a shot that day. The gun, a fine old Ithaca sixteen-gauge pump, hasn't been fired since, though I still own it. That was fifty years ago, maybe more.

Kansas spring, 1990 or so. One of my Australian Shepherds had something in her mouth, and she had that head-down, trying-to-be-unnoticed look that led me to believe I should check into this. It turned out to be a robin chick, fallen from its nest, I imagined. I opened the dog's jaws, and she dropped the robin on the grass. It seemed unharmed.

I took it and looked around for a nest but found none. Nor was there a worried mom robin flying around trying to fool us with a damaged wing act. Nothing. I was stuck with this bird. I took it inside and put it in a laundry basket. I may have had a computer at the time, but Google wasn't around yet, so I had to rely on lore that I had processed.

I knew baby robins had to be fed often. Water might be best administered from an eyedropper. Luckily, I checked with a vet and found that's a great way to drown a bird. Best to soak what it's eating, and that's all the moisture the little bird needs.

I fed the bird canned dog food in little bits, some cut-up grapes, a bug or two. It seemed to be a little eating machine.

That night, I put grass and sticks in an approximation of a nest in the laundry basket, surrounded with a towel, and expected to find a dead little carcass the next morning.

I found, instead, a healthy hungry baby bird, beak open. And vocal. I knew birds fed their young all day long, and it being a weekend, was able to accommodate the schedule. But come Monday I had to work and so did my wife. We both drove separate vehicles into the city, fifty miles north of us. I would have to take the bird with me to the advertising agency where I worked.

Soon, a routine was worked out. The bird was relatively silent if I put a towel over its laundry basket, so for the hour commute to and from work, it slept. Or whatever it did, it was quiet. Then, at work, in my office, it was fed during the day whenever it peeped. And it peeped a lot. Colleagues at the agency soon learned to be quiet around the sleeping bird, and I became known as The Birdman of Advertising.

As the robin gained weight and size, I realized it would need flying lessons and, possibly, some other education that I was ill-equipped to provide it, so I called a wildlife bureau and asked the lady what to do with a growing robin. She was aghast and told me I had ruined the bird, that it had "imprinted" on me by now, as its surrogate parent, and it had no chance to resume a normal bird life in "the wild."

She then told me this was illegal and carried a fine. When she asked for my name and address, I hung up, quietly.

The bird sat on my shoulder, on my head, on my finger. It was clear it wanted to be with me, to the consternation of my two Australian Shepherds, who were warned time and again to leave it alone. The whole thing was weighing on me. The robin needed schooling and it was only going to come from me.

It was waiting. It knew.

Early on a Saturday morning after its bird breakfast, the dogs, the bird, and I went to the front yard for flying lessons. I tossed it in the air from a kneeling position so it wouldn't fall from too great a height. It fluttered to the ground and walked around. I sighed. The dogs sat and waited. I tossed again. It fluttered again. Walked back to me. Then, the third time, it actually flew to a nearby tree that leaned and landed about three feet up on its trunk. I carefully pried it loose, tossed again, and this time it sailed around the yard a bit before it came back to me. I was holding my breath. With luck, this could be the end of my stewardship, my bird term.

I tossed it into the air again and it flew around. I left some grapes and dog food on the propane tank, plucked the bird off my shoulder, and after setting it down near the food, I went inside. I looked out the window and, horrified, saw the bird walking around on the ground and the dogs in pounce mode. I ran outside, shouting, and the bird flew to me, landing on my head. How does one teach a bird survival techniques? Flying, obviously, wasn't going to be a problem.

Fortunately, the bird found higher perches to its liking: the eaves, a tree branch. And cats didn't frequent the area because of the dogs. So it was relatively safe for the weekend. My plan for Monday was to go to work, leave the bird outside and the dogs inside, and put some food out for it. It probably would be gone when I got home. I heard a shriek from my wife.

She was in a bikini, sunning on the deck, reading a book, and the bird had landed on her toe. The shriek didn't dislodge the bird—maybe it thought it was a greeting. She was laughing now, looking at our robin. The bird wanted to be near its folks. It walked over to the dogs' water dish, took a drink, and a little fluttering dip as well.

Robins often congregated at the end of our drive, possibly for the gravel, and to dust themselves. I took her out there (we had determined her to be female), set her down on the gravel where she pecked around, and I backed away, quietly. A couple of robins landed near her, and she walked toward them. They flew away. That happened again, later. I felt as though I'd sent my kid off to the school bus and she'd been ignored, ostracized by the others at the bus stop.

The robin and I had developed our own language. I could summon her with a sort of high-pitched kissing sound that I used with the horses to get them to move. When I made the sound, she came to me, lighting on my head or shoulder. I made the sound now and she came. I wanted her to know that she would soon be one of the gang; it would all work out.

Monday morning, I laid out some food on the propane tank, said goodbye to the robin, and headed for work. I felt a mixture of liberation and guilt that day, but I lost myself in the work and the day passed soon enough. I didn't think about the bird much on the way home, distracted by city traffic, the radio, and thoughts of what I was doing at work. When I pulled into the driveway, there she was, on the front-porch eaves.

As I got out of the truck she flew to me and beat her wings, hovering about my face, and then landed on my shoulder. I put my hand near her and she perched on my finger. I got a lump in my throat thinking of her there at home all day, not knowing what had happened to her ... parents. Maybe the rude ladybird Nazi at the wildlife office was right. Maybe I would have this robin for the duration. How does one house-train a bird in the wintertime? I could see newspapers covering everything all over the house.

I needn't have worried, but as the days progressed, though she became more and more robin-like, she still waited and greeted me and my wife when we'd come home. She flew beautifully now. She would circle us and then execute a neat landing on an outstretched hand. The weekends were special times; the dogs enjoyed our company on these R&R days and so did the robin. We never named her, curiously, but she was a part of the family. When I'd be outside and wouldn't see her, I'd make the sound and there she'd be. She was fending for herself now, but I still left the occasional grape or tidbit out there for her. And she was associating with the other robins out on the gravel drive.

Well before summer was over, but on a day when the first hint of a northwest breeze alerted the senses that fall would come one day, I saw her on the fence with another, brighter red-breasted robin. The brighter-colored ones are males.

As I approached, she flew toward me. I made my noise and she flew close but didn't land. The other bird, her mate I soon determined, was obviously alarmed. He left the fence and flew erratically, making distressed sounds, and she flew back to him. Something passed between them, and she once more flew to me, circled me fairly closely, rejoined him, and they flew away together.

I knew I was losing her, but I also knew she was okay. We had imprinted on her all right, we would always be her parents, but now she was on the way to a family of her own. She wasn't attracted to other humans, so that wouldn't be a problem. And it was obvious that her new mate would lead her to more bird-like behavior. Later, I told my wife our bird had found her mate and was most probably gone.

I told her in a casual way, fairly quickly, because I had to turn away to hide an emotion that has returned to me now as I think of that moment.

I'd see the robins each spring, dusting in the gravel, and used to wonder if she was among them. Then, I checked an ornithology site and was a bit startled to find that the life span of an average robin is a little over a year. I hoped she did better than that.

It occurs to me as I glance at the Ithaca above my desk that a lot of pheasants and quail beat the odds on life span when I was the determining factor. I liked the walking and the crisp season of bird hunting. I just wasn't very good at the hunting itself.

Unmolested robins with human parents should get two years just for getting through it. After checking further, I have found that one robin lived fourteen years, and some longer than that. And I can report with some degree of certainty that I've seen ours return. The reason being that a call I used for her seemed to affect the bird in question. Not enough to approach me, but enough that it made me think it was her. Back to build another nest.

PUBLISHERS NEVER CALL

CALLER ID says it's New York. A 212 number. Could be a publisher. It's about time, the novel languishing for five or six months. Some of the sonsabitches never even email you.

"Hello?"

"Sir, good news, your doctor has ordered a Med-Call for you. You know, a system similar to the one on 'I've fallen and can't get up,' those TV ads? Well, you might even qualify to get it free, with a slight service charge ..."

"Oh no, no, no—I'll be dead in a week. I hope you will be, too."

"What? But your doctor ..."

"That loony pimp for pharma? That unspeakable fucking morphine addict? Why would you believe a wet-eyed freak so thick-tongued he can't even talk? The last time he wrote a prescription, he stabbed himself in the crotch with a Mont Blanc. That crazy guy, he's always pulling stuff like this ..."

"We'll send it to your present address and ..."

"Did I stutter, you fucking imbecile? I'm dying. He knows it. A week."

"You sound fit to me sir, in fact ..."

"What are you? A seer? A remote viewer? The Army needs you, the NSA ... oh, oh no, I, I (choking noise)." I drop the phone. It lays there.

"Sir? Sir?"

I dance my redneck dance, arms out front, causing my dogs to bark with joy. It's a dance I often do to banjo. After a while, the phone begins to buzz. I replace it in its cradle.

Publishers never call, but these rats do. All the time. Most are phony phishing attempts to get information through which they can rob you blind. Some want the money direct. A heavily- accented character told me I'd won a lottery but needed to pay taxes on it first. I asked where to send the money. This startled him, but he recovered quickly and told me to use Western Union or some wiring outfit. I said how much. He said one thousand would probably cover the nut. And that I was getting a Mercedes delivered the next day. I said "okay, I'll send the money first thing in the morning."

Sometimes, I just say, "What?" until they call me names and hang up. One "legal" caller is the Sheriff's fund. They give the so-called Sheriff's fund about one percent of what they collect. They ask me to give in memory of fallen officers and their families. I say no. They say "Don't you care?" I say "Of course." They say, "How much can we put you down for?" I say, "Nothing." So it goes. Then I either hang up or say, "What?" until they do.

Why do I answer? Boredom. Usually the landline phone rings all day and I let the answering machine pick it up. Rarely, every twenty calls or so, it's an actual call for me or my wife. But most people we know just call our cell phones. Someone calls from Jamaica about four times a day. I like their accent, so I may answer sometimes. They did leave one message; I won another lottery or sweepstakes. An international one. I've been very lucky this year.

I did actually get a call about publishing, which I took. A heavily accented though personable young woman congratulated me on one of my books, which she named, "breaking the million" barrier on Amazon.

"How depressing," I said.

"No, it's great news because now we are prepared to offer you a complete marketing program that can ..."

I was looking her up as we talked, Googling "writer scams" and coming up with her spiel almost word for word online. So I finished her speech for her in a very animated fashion and she hung up. It was a poetry book. Not even a real slick marketing plan can help a poetry book. Although, more and more young people read, perform, and write poetry these days, which is a good sign. Maybe it'll regain a place of honor as in the days of Robert Frost. Hell, he's worth a digression from this hideous subject of grimy, pot-licking, piss-willy phone scammers.

I went to see him and hear him speak once. I was about eighteen or nineteen, and he was to speak at Rockhurst College. Those were exciting days; I was being introduced to Ferlinghetti and Ginsberg, and here was the grandest of them all, the elder statesman of *real* poetry. It was winter, and I had a new camel hair overcoat that my father had bought me for Christmas at a Plaza store in KC, an Ivy League haberdashery. I felt pretty spiffy. It was probably worth more than my car, a 1949 Ford with loud pipes. I settled in, in the upper balcony's loge and enjoyed a night of a legend sharing poetry and anecdotes. He was pretty funny; I hadn't expected that. At the end, the host, a bishop or something in robes and a sort of fledgling pope's hat, said, "I will pass out first. Mr. Frost will pass out after me, and you will all please wait to pass out after us."

Frost leans over to the microphone and says, "Must be all that communion wine. I'm usually the first one to pass out."

We roared. We loved him for that, for his no-BS style and his outsized talent, his quick humor, and ... well, I rather imagine publishers *did* call him. Often.

Must run. Publishers Clearing House is leaving a message. Must be from their Pakistani office. I can hardly understand it, but I've won, I know that much.

THE MANGLED EMMY

LET ME START with a disclaimer. Any advice I give is worth just what you pay for it. What do I know? I drive a fifteen-year-old pickup and my last royalty check was for twelve dollars.

But during a tumultuous advertising career, I won more than two-hundred awards. Enough chrome and Lucite to make a couple of Buicks, and some were even meaningful. Like the one for a literacy campaign. That got a Presidential Citation. Maybe Carter or Lyndon or one of them. I wasn't big on politics. Nor am I now, luckily.

An Emmy. Some say it was only a Midwest Emmy, and that's true. It was for a TV commercial, to which I contributed little. But, believe me, an Emmy is an Emmy, especially when it gets mangled by window washers who knocked it around in my office. This Emmy looks like a for-real Emmy only the base is smaller. And when I complained to the management about its demise, they said they'd replace it.

It took about a year, due to various provenance measures and serial number mistakes, but I finally got it replaced. They had to have the damaged one back. So it's a very real Emmy. The director entered the commercial into the competition and I'm glad he did. I feel a little less like a fraud when I look at it.

From the day I left a paving company, an adult job, and went into advertising, my dream job, I've felt a bit like an impostor. I dealt in alleged ideas. I climbed from a crowded artist bullpen into the Creative Director's office and perched there, perilously, for years.

No advice so far, but that of persistence. Persist, whatever the job. Get a bump up if possible. Think of it as your Oscar journey, no matter where you are. Perhaps Burger King or maybe a Chicken costume handing out leaflets.

I freelanced in L.A., talk about perilous. I won't go into that crazy interim, but I eventually landed a creative group head spot at Dancer Fitzgerald Sample which became DFS Dorland which became Saatchi & Saatchi. I made it through those seas of change writing Toyota print and broadcast. With time on my hands, I wrote other things.

I wrote a screenplay adaptation of a colleague's novel that had the same guy who'd brought *Zen and the Art of Motorcycle Maintenance* to the world for its agent. He liked the screenplay, suggested a different beginning, and then he passed away prematurely. The screenplay went nowhere, and the book didn't make its advance.

I wrote treatments. Sent them to Cannes with a friend. One got us meetings in rooms with shiny conference tables. It went away. I was asked if I was interested in writing a book about the turnaround of a famous motorcycle company. I felt I'd have to quit my day job. They felt I wanted too much. It went away. A screenplay went to a semi-famous actor who had expressed interest in it. It went away.

Then I went away.

I got homesick. I wanted a couple of horses like I'd had for half my life. Maybe a double-wide. I had some savings, a pittance in L.A., but a little poke of gold dust in Kansas. I found a one-hundred-year-old farmhouse. A creative director job in KC And I persisted.

But like you, I'm assuming, I never forgot that Hollywood sign. The Toyota shoots were as close as I got, but they were a great placeholder for my eventual screenwriting credits scrolling down as everyone but me leaves the theater. And in KC, I got some Best of Shows for radio, radio my training had made visual. TV. Print. A few more awards.

I moved on to another Creative Director position, got old, and retired. I wrote books. I produced a lot of welded-steel sculptures. I outlived a dozen horses, some fine dogs. I still write. I still sculpt. And, you know what? I persist. My books are visual. One I'm writing now will make a helluva feature film. It takes place in L.A. and a logline might be: A young boxer defies his mob owners and refuses to lose an upcoming fight. He becomes a killer by default, a landscaper by capability, and a private eye by choice. Stranger things have happened. On second thought: no, they haven't. Present-day L.A. is the locale.

So you see, I'm still dreaming. Once I get *L.A. Hardscape* published, then I'll shop it around as a possible feature film. Like I push *Ruined Days* now and then. It's on Amazon with some short story collections and poetry books I wrote.

Luck. Perseverance. Maybe some talent, but that's subjective. But here's the good news (for you). If you're reading this because you're affiliated with Stage 32,[1] you're probably a whole lot more connected to the industry than I was, or am. I cope with Adult-Onset Optimism daily, and I know I'll get at least a corner of my dream before I'm done. But whether you're a film student at UCLA, a lighting tech in Minneapolis, or an actress in Austin, you're oh, so close.

My uncle Reno Pete said, "Stay in the action. Even if you're playing with scared money. *Especially* if you're playing with

---

1 Written as a blog for *Stage 32*.

scared money. It's just chips." And "my" Emmy? It's still an Emmy. Set your sights. Emmys and Oscars and those other glittering trophies will all have names on them. Might as well be yours. Stage 32 is where a lot of action takes place to help get you there.

AN OVERDUE LOVE LETTER TO TENSAS PARISH

I'VE BEEN TOLD the Manhattan Project had nothing to do with Manhattan yet there we were, 120th Street on the cusp of Harlem during WWII, and my stepfather was doing something secret for the war effort.

We had taken the train from Kansas City. A marvelous adventure with sleeping cars, dining cars, heavy silverware on starched linen, racing with the trees, cornfields, the moon. We'd left one huge, cavernous station with shafts of light pouring through high windows to marble floors, noise, public address announcements, Fred Harvey restaurants, for another, even larger cavernous station. We ate from little windows that had pieces of pie and sandwiches in them. You released them with coins. It was my first lesson in economics. If I had coins, I could eat.

I recall a brownstone, a walk-up apartment, hall walls that smelled of old cooking, and playing on the front stoop. We were in financial straits, I remember that, and when I fell asleep on the city bus from a preschool—Barnard they have since told me—I ended up at the end of the line, and they had to send a cab to get me. A needless expense. I also recall sheets hung dividing a small room, for some degree of privacy. And pizza, known then as pizza pie. Some sort of celebration. Shortly thereafter, I was in St. Joseph, Louisiana and the folks were elsewhere. Recently married, I can understand their desire to be the hell away from kids. I get that now. I didn't then.

And moving from New York to Tensas Parish, Louisiana was not simply culture shock; it was a drop-forged blitzkrieg, mamma jamma, ding-dong whiplash. With extra blasting caps. And I grew to love it.

Before I continue, let me set the record straight about the name, Manhattan Project. It did, indeed, get its start in Manhattan. I refer you to "Why They Called It the Manhattan Project" by William Broad, from *The New York Times*, October 30, 2007. And that's that. Google it. And that Mensa guy in Los Angeles who told me, "You know, of course, the Manhattan Project got its start at the University of Chicago. It had nothing to do with Manhattan Island." Even Mensans can be wrong.

But that's not the story here. My stepfather was some kind of genius, speaking of Mensa. (The Los Angeles guy had a license plate that said, yep, MENSA. It's okay to roll your eyeballs.) Long gone, my stepfather remains in my mind as The Atomic Bomb Guy. And his father, the Episcopal minister, will forever be Pop. He's the reason The Atomic Bomb Guy was so smart. Mother B., my stepgrandmother, had a formative role in that she chopped off chickens' heads in the front yard, impressing me with the set of her mouth which was similar to when I tried out some talk learned in town. The line I repeated was something like, "C'mere a minute ago sumbitch, gimme orange pop, n'est-ce pas?" I liked the rhythm of it, the exotic flavor, the fractured imperative. I can still taste the Lava soap, feel the grit of it on my tongue. It was clear that my efforts to fit in were flawed. But Pop, much as I liked him, was no help on my elocutionary tightrope. He said things like "That's too dear," to mean too expensive. That kind of talk would get you beat up in town or on the gravel roads and bayou fringes where I loitered.

I got the sense his congregation liked him a lot, liked his English roots. Episcopal Church was not dissimilar from Catholic Mass, lots of kneeling, rising, chanting, swinging of the thurible. If I'm anything, I'm Episcopal, though I was baptized in a Catholic Church. Oddly I don't remember Pop *in* church in St. Joe, though it's a safe bet I was present. I believe I slept a good deal during service. I do remember him fishing, tying flies, raising exotic orchids, working on things in his shop, dealing with the family dogs, one of which killed our chickens and the neighbors' as well on a blood spree. He had lots of books and got more in the mail, and Mother B. would chide him about those, saying we could barely afford to eat much less pay C.O.D. for expensive books. He had once invented something that was bought and used by Coleman Products, in their lanterns I believe, and was often working with small electric motors and magnetic gadgets in his shop.

He poured me lead soldiers in a mold, the lead heated over a Bunsen burner in his workshop, and we painted them in their appropriate regimental colors. And I vividly remember listening to war news on the radio in the evening while playing with small colorful tins that smelled of their original spices, toffees, and exotic contents, tins from England. I played with these in lieu of metal cars and steam shovels which had become almost extinct due to the war, steel being at a premium.

My Yankeeness faded as the war dragged on, and I began to appreciate Tensas Parish as an idyllic playground and, later, a rich contributor to whatever creative aims I have. A poem I wrote about St. Joe, one of many, may convey the flavor of the place as well as anything I could say in prose:

Bad Bull Shortcut

Catty corner through a pasture
made the bayou a quicker walk
but when the bull was there the
boy didn't take the dare, squared

the fence's rusty barbed wire.
Pasture's edge was in a swamp
and an army of cypress trees
put their roots and knees where

alligators sometimes flashed in
shallows of the black waters
and garfish swam, merganzers
flew and fallen trees made okay

bridges though slick with moss
and droppings. Back to the bull.
He grazed, his sight curtailed by
primitive goggles allowing only

slits of light and now and then
a bit of boy's jeans and striped
T-shirt, enough to paw the earth
and try to lumber over slowly

and the boy was looking for
the figures made of wood and
paint and bike reflectors, with
biblical phrases painted on the

barkless, naked faded trunks
in misspelled words like Hore
and Kign and Revelatun Fore
and backwards Ns and Ss that

were more apocalyptic than
the message, more deliciously
absorbed and more a source
of wonder to the big eyed boy.

    About those figures made of wood and paint and reflectors. Were they the creations of a bayou resident? A town artist? A bored farmer or a mad swamp hermit? When I try to remember their shapes, they waver like heat on a blacktop road and disappear. And am I conflating the words on them with "The Sign Painter" of Calloway County in Fulton, Missouri? That's where I attended Westminster College before moving on to the University of Arkansas. Those signs we derided as smartass college kids are now in a permanent collection at the Kansas City Art Institute. The signs were everywhere on a rural property, wonderful streams of consciousness about politics, religion, sin, hypocrisy, and the unfairness of the ruling elite. These days, with cellphone photography, I would have a record of them. I secretly loved them. The usual motif was black letters on a white board, sometimes embellished with a word in color for emphasis. He called PhDs "Pickled Hog Dates," and some of the professors at Westminster had their integrity impugned by these very public statements. The sign painter called a spade a spade, and a college degree was a useless set of initials that deserved contempt.

In Tensas Parish, I was more open to folk art, true art, than in later years when, in my callow search for sophistication, I regarded it as crude. My world has turned a few thousand degrees since then, and I see it, this so-called outsider art, as the one true, unaffected art. Straight out of the psyche, unadulterated, beautiful in its guilelessness.

The sculpture I'm doing now, the Tensas Parish series, is an attempt to capture some of that undissembling by allowing the work to follow its own path, starting with dead, barkless tree trunks and branches. The same sort of stark fingers one sees reaching out of a lake or slough. I'm a welder, so that part of the work is affixing "collars" and various colored metals to the trunks. No cypress knees here in Kansas, but that would be going too far in my opinion; the shapes and colors are what will bring some of that boyhood awe back. I'm not trying to recreate the pieces. Even if I could, that would constitute copying, and that's not art nor would it be fair to the whole "folk art" movement. Could be what I'm making isn't art either. I like to think it is. It moves me on several levels. Perhaps it will move others who view it and trigger a feeling of recurrence or even déjà vu that would be ideal. To have that same shadowy vaporous feeling I have. Then I will have done what I set out to do. A causation of "primal." Or, at least, a feeling of genuineness. Maybe ... maybe even beauty, in its way. Forgive me if I insert a poem here; again, I think it actually might clarify what I'm struggling with.

Come and See

In Tensas Parish a small boy is drawn to
a structure partly hidden by the bayou mist
of morning. He approaches with something
like trepidation mixed with good shivers.

The thing stands about eight feet high and
it could be a cypress rooted tree but for its
three-pronged rusty steel legs of base, then
the trunk is smooth, white, and painted in

evenly-spaced rings deep blue fresh green
a lavender, and collars of steel are affixed
to it, some with chrome sun igniters, glass
exciters reflect the coming light through

the mist and it changes as the sun grows
hot and picks red glass to shift and spit
out messages of mirrored telegraphy and
other urgencies that draw the boy near.

Near enough to touch it but he doesn't as
some atavistic god reverence tells him no
because he might become another light
another ring another band of rust a part

of this thing that calls to something deep in
him, *come and see*, as in Revelations 6 and
when seen, cannot be wished away but still
it pulls him to its dream-lit misting mantle.

Perfectly clear now, right? Well, maybe the pieces won't need explanation. Good stuff doesn't. I'd love it if this was good stuff, the Tensas Parish pieces, but I have no more confidence in my work than the first time I sat and painted on a blank canvas board at art school. Every time out it's that way, but then I get lost in the work and it's no longer a thing. What happens happens. I think it's harder than when I'm doing a horse or a crow; at least I have something to go by with a sculpture that looks like something familiar.

Anyway, this isn't about the sculpture; it's about St. Joe. Tensas Parish. It never occurred to me to ask Pop why they called it Tensas Parish instead of Tensas County. It was just his parish, that's all. I assumed the other pastors and preachers felt it was *their* parish. Then I heard why Louisiana did that while no other states did. One reason: Louisiana is unlike any other state. It's a magical place with its Huey Longs and its biggest gushers in the world and its shrimpers and Cajuns and Spanish moss.

Parishes: Louisiana was officially Roman Catholic under both France's and Spain's rule—the ecclesiastical term was never in question for boundaries, and in 1807 when the territorial government took over, parish stuck. Only Louisiana does this. It's part of her character, and she's got a lot of it, god love her.

Pop, a nonsmoker, had a congregation at a wealthy church in a North Carolina cigarette town. Until a well-dressed parishioner approached him after the service and offered him a Lucky Strike cigarette. "Not a cough in a carload," piped the gent. (This may be apocryphal, as it was Old Gold's slogan—but the American Tobacco VP who said it may have applied it to all of the company's products) Pop refused the offer and said, "Maybe not, but surely another nail in your coffin."

No doubt he was pleased with his homophonic riposte, meant in humor. But it resulted in his immediate demotion to the lower slobbovia of Episcopal churchdom: St. Joseph, Louisiana. Tensas Parish was then, and is now, the least-inhabited parish in the state of Louisiana.

I heard the story in a sort of aural dyslexia when the Atomic Bomb Guy told my mom about it. Coffins in Carloads is how I heard it. But the meaning was clear. When The Man offers you a Lucky, take it and don't smart off. Otherwise, they send you to the swamps. And that's where I was going for the duration. No one had even offered me a cigarette, but I was sentenced along with Pop and Mother B.

Man I was lucky. I was as free in St. Joe as I'll ever be in this life. And warm. Even in winter. Even on deliciously stormy days when the lights flickered and the treetops circled in a troubled and bruised sky. I wandered everywhere. Sometimes, looking for my comic book (funny book, I was often reminded by a large young fellow my age who punched me for emphasis—I soon got it right) hero, The Heap. I knew he was around here, the comic, oops, funny book said so. Louisiana bayou. The Heap was a downed Luftwaffe pilot who had turned against the evil Nazis. His body moldered into a sort of leaf pile of swamp detritus, and he walked about, slogged into scenes of bad people tying women to sawmills and the like, and he saved them. Then he would embrace the bad guy and take him into his ever-growing pile of swamp trash, compost him into himself, and disappear. I had the visual reference on this character, so I'd recognize him when I saw him and harbored no doubts as to his reality. Pop said, "Well, if you see him, don't bring him around here."

The bayou, to me, was a place of magic. Often low-lit and canopied with swags of moss and ancient-growth tupelo and cypress trees. Once, I ventured into a spongy area that smelled so bad I thought it must be the lair of The Heap, my own personal Sasquatch. As I drew closer, the smell grew worse. Then I saw an unforgettable tableau: a large shape, legs up, and buzzards walking around it. They looked like small old men in overcoats. I ran all the way home. Pop said it was a cow, just old and gone in there to die. And what was I doing in there anyway.

I remember cotton fields, people working in them. Sometimes, they sang. It looked like interesting work to me, and more so when I heard they got paid by the bag. So many bags equaled a Schwinn with a chrome rack on the back fender, to me. A Red Ryder BB gun. A Velocette motorcycle in one of Pop's *Popular Mechanics*. Pop said I was too young to pick cotton, but we'd see about it when I was older. I never felt the pain in the back, the legs, the sun-torched neck, the bleeding hands. It remained a romantic notion to me until I met a man from Texas, a distinguished artist, whose parents had been cotton-picking champions in his town, the same town that Willie Nelson was from, and who had picked cotton himself. He said it was "have-to" work. If you didn't have to, you wouldn't do it. I did plenty of that kind of work as a laborer in construction later on.

Tensas Parish people, in my memory, were friendly and humorous, the grown-ups anyway. It took me a while to crack the code of my contemporaries. My real father was in the service, a radioman in the Navy. But my stepfather (Bumsted, the Atomic Bomb Man) and mother were a mystery to me. I wasn't at all sure what the arrangement was. I did know, when asked if I wanted the name Bumsted added to my already cumbersome Guinotte, that it was a quick nope. I liked Dagwood and Blondie in the comic section, oops, the funny papers, but I didn't want to be in there with them. I was one step removed, living with Pop and Mother B. The other kids just thought of me as an orphan or a kid nobody wanted from up North. That was fine with me. Attaining detente with my age group was my survival aim. That accomplished, the countryside was mine. And what a countryside. I'm proud to have been a tiny part of that Mississippi River Delta area of St. Joseph, Louisiana. Where is it? Just twenty minutes from Waterproof, I learned to say. Same side of the river. Where a small boy absorbed the magic and appreciates it still.

CHICKENS ONE DAY, FEATHERS THE NEXT

Rudy used to say that. "Chickens one day, feathers the next." About people who had died. Maybe they had disappointed him, dying before their time, in his estimation. Or, when he said it of people he didn't know, it was a way of saying fuck death. A. Rudolph Green was a tough little guy. A banty from East St. Louis. But *actually* tough, not playing at it. I met him at Westminster College in Fulton, Missouri, where Churchill made his famed Iron Curtain speech. It was our freshman year. Student loans were not a thing in the late fifties, and to get by we both worked at Gene Miller's Phillips 66 station after classes. No one pumped their own gas then, service stations earned the title. We pumped gas, fixed flats, changed oil, took trash to the dump, worked pretty hard, and we became good friends. I had a primered 1949 Ford with loud pipes and some speed equipment. Rudy had a flashy 1955 Chevy convertible, red and white, lowered pipes. This was in 1957.

Gene allowed us to bring in a six-pack on Saturdays, and we put in a full day, having a cold beer at noon with a sandwich. Those were simple times, good times. We were more tolerated by the townies than the "cake-eaters" or wealthier students at the college because we worked and because our cars weren't stock.

We both took R.O.T.C. at Westminster. Rudy advised me it was a good idea in case I was ever going to join the military, so I did. We marched, cleaned our M-1s, had tests. Then Rudy joined the Marines our sophomore year. We stayed up one night drinking and talking. He made the decision, and I was to accompany him the next morning to the recruiter. I overslept. Rudy didn't.

We wrote often. I went on to the University of Arkansas, then the Kansas City Art Institute, got married. I was 2S and had a lottery number that never came up. Rudy had been in Salvador and some places he described to me in letters. Vietnam became a familiar name, civil rights, the protests, the turmoil. Though he was a Catholic and felt deeply about it, Rudy said, "Chickens one day, feathers the next," about JFK. Our own government, in no less august guise than the United States House Select Committee on Assassinations, admitted it was "probably" a conspiracy. Innocence was in short supply as we grew up and older. Then it ran out completely and got replaced with a cynical sort of accidie.

Rudy visited us in Iowa, stayed a few days. He was rising in the USMC. He drove a Jaguar E-Type, a green convertible, and allowed my little kids to steer it while sitting on his lap. They called him Uncle Rudy and marveled at him. He'd been wounded once, recovered, did another tour after that.

Up late, drinking, he told me an odd thing; he said he couldn't wait to get back. He said, I remember, about my career as an advertising art director: "Look, you're really good at what you do, and you dig it. Nothing's better than being good at something and doing it for a living. I'm good at what I do. And I want to get back there, doing it."

He told me about when he was wounded, having lain there but still holding his weapon, and when two Charleys, as he called them, advanced on him. Laughing, he said, "I got them right between the running lights." Then the chickens and feathers comment. It was the last time I ever saw him.

He did three tours, wounded twice. They were going to give him a desk job so he quit, retired as a Captain. He wrote me that he and some buddies had bought into a ski resort in California and that he was now working in the "ethical drug" business out there. They called it that back before big pharma couldn't really lay claim to the term anymore. Then when I didn't hear from him for a long spell, I wrote his parents.

His father told me that Rudy was in Fresno, and someone tried to jack his car. Of course Rudy wasn't having that. He was shot in the face and died instantly. The person who killed him was caught.

Wounded twice, three tours in Vietnam, and he died at the hands of a garbage bag just as he was entering a phase of his life that could have been the best ever.

I never really got over it. Half a century since then. At one time I fantasized, or maybe seriously planned, to wait until the person was released. So many of these people do ten years and get out. I tried to get information from the Fresno P.D. and California Corrections without success. I thought about hiring a private detective. And all the time I knew it wouldn't even any scores; it was fruitless, stupid.

The reason I know I never really got over it is what happened this morning on my farm. I went to feed and water a rooster that took up residence in the horses' loafing shed about a month ago. Some free-range peacocks, peahens, and another rooster come daily, and I put out some chicken scratch, dry dog food, and leftover greens. They expect it now. But they all go home at sundown. "My" rooster has no place to go. Except the loafing shed. He roosts on the horses' hay rack, fairly high off the ground.

Eddie didn't crow yesterday. (Eddie Arcaro was his name, for the marvelous call he made, *Ar-Car-oooo*) He was strangely silent. But he ate well and drank water, seemed fine. I went online and looked up why roosters might not crow, and one answer was that a rooster would be silent when he didn't want to bring attention to himself. That day, I'd seen a gray form near the loafing shed and ran to see what it was. I thought, the way it moved, it was a possum and don't like them around because they carry a disease that horses can get. So I banged around out there until I was sure it was gone. It may have been a bobcat or a raccoon, but I didn't think of that then.

This morning Eddie didn't show for his food. He usually came up on the deck and crowed for me to come feed him.

I went to the corral and saw the white feathers everywhere. He'd put up a fight but was no match for whatever predator came for him. I sat down in the packed dirt of the corral and picked up some feathers. I felt very tired.

As I sat there among the blowing feathers I thought of Rudy and his saying. And I am hurting for Eddie. And for Rudy. Poles apart, a fowl and a human, right?

The feathers, man. The fucking feathers. I gathered them in a shoebox to bury. And I will keep two. One for Eddie. One for Rudy.

IT'S A TULSA
KIND OF DAY ...

with addendum after hearing of The Greenwood Massacre of 1921 at age eighty

I SAY THAT to the pups when several things coincide and mesh. It's a sunny day of moderate temperature and the sky is blue and cloudless. It can be spring, summer, any time of year, really, but usually green and budding. The synaptic ingredient that brings this together is a piston aircraft, the sound, then the sight of a small, silvery light airplane against the blue, making its way across that limitless canopy. And I am pleasantly warmed as though by a drug. Every time.

"It's a Tulsa kind of day, guys." I say this to Cash and Millie, as I've said it to Rocket and Lucy before them, and Jack and Mickey before them. They look at me and smile, continue what they were about, nose-reading trails of animals, trying to catch a butterfly, exploring here and there in their home pastures.

I am transported back to Tulsa in the best years of its life, the late forties and the fifties. School is out and I am anticipating being sent to Kansas City to spend the summer with my paternal grandmother, my aunt, and my father. These KC summers were a balm, low stress, good food, plenty of RC Cola, fresh-baked chocolate chip cookies, lemonade on the screened-in porch, freedom of movement such as I'd never known. But Tulsa was the point of departure, the gateway, the sunrise. It was a boomtown back then, exciting and full of promises. A scene comes to mind: it is dusk, and some sort of activity animates the neighborhood, a party, a barbecue, maybe a nearby block party, I don't quite remember. But I do recall some older kids my sister's age making their kinetic kind of commotion, always exciting to me. And there is an old jalopy, a 1937 Ford I think—I was into automobiles back then as now—and it careens around the corner near our house, and it turns over. Slides along on its bulbous fenders, throwing sparks in the early evening.

Two boys extricate themselves, boys with T-shirts and ducktail haircuts, short on top in a flattop, like all of my teen heroes. They are laughing and talking excitedly as they climb out the doorway of the side that is up. They apply themselves to the top of the car and begin lifting and rocking it. A curious group is forming, and some of them help, and then the car is upright again. The starter grinds, catches, a small cheer goes up, and the car speeds away as night descends. The group of onlookers dissipates, devolves back to the party or previous activity.

That was Tulsa, then, to me. It typified an attitude, an air of recklessness without consequence, fun. I couldn't have put it in words then, except to say, *that's Tulsa*. That right there, what just happened.

Tulsa was also an open pink Jeep with *CADIJAH* stenciled on the hood in black capital letters. It stopped at our house one day. I watched from the top of our terraced lawn, girls, contemporaries of my sister, classmates at Holland

Hall, the school she attended, spilled out, Emmylu hurried down to meet them. Cadijah Helmerich was the driver. Her brother, Walter, was to marry Peggy Dow, a Hollywood starlet, that summer. The elder Helmerichs were drilling-tool millionaires. The movie magazines stated that Peggy Dow was marrying an "Oklahoma oil driller." This was Tulsa. Glamour. Excitement. Buzz. Here I was on the periphery of all this. Infected by that feeling,

That day, or soon after, an open light aircraft flew low over the neighborhoods dropping clouds of leaflets. I followed on my bicycle, skidding to stop and pick up some of the magical papers from the sky. Other kids were doing the same. So were adults on lawns, in the streets, in parking lots. They were advertisements, of course, but serially numbered for prizes like a car, lawnmowers, items at stores in Utica Square. Free services at cleaners, where I hauled wagons full of hangers collected door to door to sell at two for a penny, back to the cleaners who had spawned them. Garden tools at the hardware store. Trips from the travel agent. Utica Square was a Helmerich enterprise, and one of my favorite places to go on my bicycle. A Tulsa day often included Utica Square, and a friend of mine and I would go there to make money. We shined shoes there, boots of oil men. The tips were good and we spent them at the drugstore on chocolate root beers and comic books.

My collection of leaflets won nothing that I recall, but the fact they came from the sky, from a low-flying light aircraft buzzing our neighborhood, that was part of the magic carpet fabric of a Tulsa Day.

Sometimes, two or three of us would hike over to the rose gardens at Woodward Park and play among the statuary, fountains, mazes. Those were days when being gone all day, morning to dusk, caused no alarm to parents.

Especially mine, who were relieved to have me out of sight and mind. Saturdays and summer days were all like that to my memory. Traipsing in a group to the Philbrook Museum to look at the cowboy regalia, climb the rocks on the hills below it, try to catch frogs in the small waterfalls and natural creeks.

Saturdays were serial days at the small movie house nearby, cowboy cliffhangers to get you back the following weekend. After the film we'd swagger out into the sunshine, slit-eyed and tough, conjecturing how the ranger was going to escape from torture and death at the hands of the mad-dog killer, Slade. This might be it for the ranger this time.

Then we'd gather around the Filipino yo-yo champion (champ of the Philippines? The world, maybe?) who waited outside the theater and watch him do impossible tricks with wooden Duncan yo-yos. If we had enough money left over from the movies, we'd buy a yo-yo and he, the champion, would flick open a small knife and carve a bird on it for an extra few cents. He wore a jean jacket with yo-yo brands on it and a jeweled *CHAMPION* in an arch on the back. He was a virtuoso, a true master, magician of string and wood sleight of hand. We'd forget about the ranger's plight and work at Walk the Dog. A kid would warn me not to do that on the sidewalk or I'd ruin the bird the champ had carved on the side. I saw his point, this kid with a wiser mind than mine, and I'd practice on the grass.

With whirring yo-yos shooting out in front of us, returning with a stinging slap to the hand, we'd mosey ranger-like along the sidewalk, until a window display would catch our eye. "Loud as a cap gun, but uses plain paper rolls instead of expensive caps!" Our mouths would drop open, yo-yos bobbing forgotten, as we eyed the savage-looking squared-off paper popper, with its large trigger that conformed to the grip of what might be a ray gun. Cold gray with red accents, it glittered in the window of the dime store. "Only $1.50!" We vowed to somehow have scraped up an extra dollar and a half the following Saturday, if we could even wait that long.

Caddying at Southern Hills Country Club would do it. But the bus ride cost money and the older kids all got the first golfers and best tippers. Chancy. Hangers were too slow. Too low-paying. Setting pins at the bowling alley was good but dangerous, and you had to know someone and pay an older kid vigorish. Shining shoes and boots at Utica Square, but it was spotty—you could go hours without a taker.

Shagging golf balls at the driving range! A quarter a bucket. Walking distance through the woods from my house, and there were always golf balls in the woods on the way. Six buckets would get me the paper popper ray gun. I would start that day.

The Studebaker sat in the driveway, the car that detractors claimed they couldn't tell if it was coming or going. Someone was home. Should I risk getting snared into a no-pay leaf raking type of chore that would consume an hour? I wanted a sandwich but would just do without in order to get to the driving range unimpeded. I stopped in the detached garage for a receptacle for collecting balls in the woods on the way. I found a cardboard box full of brass plumbing parts, dumped them and hurried to the woods.

Hawkeyed and Indian-like I moved silently through the woods, scaring up a rabbit, a small covey of quail. I fired an imaginary ray gun at them, bringing down several for dinner that night.

I found three golf balls, two of which were so scarred and weathered, Mr. Bradley would never accept them in a bucket. He dumped buckets out to make sure you hadn't salted them with dirt clods. I found more as I neared the sound of clubs whipping through the air, the smack of the ball.

"Go out beyond the two-hundred-yard marker, get them balls way out in the weeds and boonies where the machine picker don't go," Mr. Bradley said. "You get hit, it ain't my fault, hear?"

I took four buckets and my box.

Two hours and sixty-five cents later (three buckets, one of which was not full) I gave up and headed home, thirsty and discouraged. I could spend a dime or so at the drugstore for a chocolate root beer. I'd still be fifty cents up on my ray gun quota. But I couldn't just ride over there and get the gun tomorrow as I'd planned. Maybe an advance on my allowance. Or did I already have one? Or two?

I borrowed against a future allowance and got the gun the next day. It didn't keep my interest for long and joined other abandoned toys in a corner of my room. We are an acquisitional culture. But the must-haves don't fulfill. Maybe a Lamborghini does, but I'll never know. Besides, I was on the cusp of teenhood and beginning to feel that cap guns and paper popper ray guns were for younger boys. This feeling would come and go, but fewer of us were exhibiting the full suspension of disbelief it took to be cops and robbers, cowboys and Indians. We took that to the movies with us and hid it well.

I was still a Boy Scout, but not for long. The Scoutmaster's kid was magically achieving a full complement of badges and plateaus while I was languishing behind. I had some merit badges for woodwork and a couple of inconsequentials. We went on a twenty-mile hike, and I had my regulation canteen and an apple, a Baby Ruth, and a sandwich in my pack but still wasn't very prepared. My hiking shoes were the battered penny loafers I wore to school. The Scoutmaster said, "You'll never make it in those," and shook his head ruefully. He was outfitted, like his kid, in full regalia: hiking shorts, combat boots, and a sash with many badges sewn on. I fell behind them and walked with a couple of my friends who wore jeans and P.F. Flyers, school stuff. We passed the Scoutmaster twelve miles later, sitting and waiting for the car patrol to notify his wife to come and pick him up. His boots and socks sat beside him while he nursed some ugly blisters on his heels. That was a Tulsa kind of day. Clear blue sky, a piston plane buzzing somewhere. The twenty miles were full of pastures, creeks, woods, but mostly hard-surfaced roads marked with flags and numbers. Pretty boring, actually. We stopped and ate when we felt like it and had some laughs at the Scoutmaster's expense.

"You'll never make it in those," I barked, pointing at my friends' sneakers.

I made the twenty-mile marker along with my sneaker-shod friends and made plans to drop scouts from my activities. I didn't announce it to my parents, I just quit going. Nothing was ever said about it. I'd never be an Eagle Scout, but some things simply have to be jettisoned in the hard decision-making process. It was just too damned hard to get all those merit badges.

As for confirmation in the Episcopal Church, just quitting wasn't an option. *Matthew, Mark, Luke, John, The Acts* became *Matthew Mark, Look John, The Axe!* in order to memorize, and other such mnemonic devices barely got me through it, though I suspect anyone got confirmed in order to become an upstanding dues-paying adult member putting their kids through the same thing.

Sometimes, we'd take the bus downtown, for a movie, Orange Julius, donuts. I didn't know it then, but I was at ground zero of some of the most infectious Art Deco in the United States. Oil tycoons had latched onto the style at the height of its popularity and incorporated it into the prairie skyscrapers and every corner of the city. To this day I carry the germ. It has crept into my art direction in advertising, and when I gaze around our cluttered farmhouse, I see radios, seltzers, statuary, stained glass, paintings, framed pieces, even a bumper car, doorknobs, pens—all Art Deco, some Art Moderne, and other movements of the period. Sometimes, it's a Tulsa kind of day when my eye focuses on an old Art Deco movie camera gathering dust on the kitchen island. Or a period fan atop the refrigerator. Or a red hand-cranked rocket-shaped juicer affixed to the wall near a faded Grapette mirror. But there's probably an airplane just within my hearing, and sun slanting in through Venetian blinds. Certain things must aggregate to make a Tulsa day.

It can be an elevator door in the music hall in Downtown Kansas City, one of those very ornate, gold-leaf Art Deco doors. But other things must occur. Sun on the marble floor. The buzz of a plane outside. I am afflicted, but specifically so. The plane brings it on, or brings it together, like the onset of an epileptic seizure being caused by flashing lights or musical sounds.

The low-buzzing leaflet plane figures into it, of course. I built model planes after that, and as I grew older and more adept, the planes became larger and more sophisticated. Then they stopped. Motorcycles and cars replaced the planes. But the Tulsa Days never forsook. And the plane remains a symbol, I might suppose, of freedom, of discovery, of wonder.

I kissed my first girl in Tulsa. Her name was Diane. It was a clumsy moment, as such moments often are, but it worked out well. She didn't run screaming or rebuff me. She liked me well enough to wear my ID bracelet, as was the fashion then, and may still have it today. It was a heavy piece, silver, with *GVINOTTE* engraved in capital letters. When I pointed out to the jeweler that it should be a U, not a V, he said the V was an old Roman usage of U. I wished then that I had used my nickname, Butch, but so many years later I realize that with my way of printing then, it would have read *BVTCH*. And I knew adults were always right. No use arguing. I lived with the *GVINOTTE* ID but it was always a bit lacking to me. Never quite right. Diane never questioned it, not that I recall.

The movie *TULSA* had its premiere in Tulsa about this time. Just as I felt the town couldn't get any more exciting, it did. The day of the premiere, there was a parade and I was there. I never missed filling-station openings, how could I miss this? Susan Hayward, Robert Preston, Chill Wills, rode by in separate convertibles, and Chill Wills handed me a studio eight by ten black-and-white publicity photo as I ran alongside. It was inscribed, "Hi, Cuz!" He called everyone "cousin" and somehow, in my mind, this became familial, and he a blood relative. Chill Wills and I were cousins. I also thought it never rained on Easter.

Today, in Kansas, it's a gray, windy February day. The bare trees are moving at their tops. Colors are muted. No planes fly. Don't get me wrong—good to great things can occur on such a day, just not the added blithe transport of Tulsa-ness. That's reserved for special times.

addendum to this fond memory—an indelible blight

I was blissfully unaware of Greenwood, The Black Wall Street of Tulsa, and the horrific massacre of 1921, from childhood all the way to my eighties, or I'd never have written such a piece. I leave it here because until I learned about this vile event, Tulsa occupied a magical place in my mind that released endorphins or seemed to. Now it doesn't. I don't want to forget that place, fictional as it may now be. The racists can't take away my childhood, as they did thousands of others, but past sins have a way of becoming ulcerous.

Such a well-kept secret and I can see why, surely, over the years, few white Tulsans would even acknowledge it. But it festered and broke through, and to Tulsa's somewhat delayed credit, the city is taking it on and struggling with it.

I recommend Public TV's *Tulsa* to begin to understand the horror and the tormenting aftermath. It is one of the more compelling cases for reparations in the many that this country has bred. No one taught such things in school; local history, the history of Indigenous, Black, and otherwise was *tabula rasa* and quickly glossed over. We know that now. Slavery alone teaches us an inextinguishable lesson in man's capacity for accommodating evil, but we know that, too. Huge questions remain, and I can't address them here in a short addendum.

Greenwood. It would be easier to say rabble took over; ignorant poor whites intent on revenge for Blacks living well. But this awful chapter in Tulsa's history was actually encouraged by the city fathers, egged on by incendiary articles in *The Tulsa Tribune*. Any understanding of the conflagration has to do with deeper demons of fear and greed and pride, murderous when gathered and ignited and fanned. There were demons at work here.

Look up *The Public Domain Review* online and type in "Photographing the Tulsa Massacre of 1921," an essay by Karlos K. Hill, and steel yourself for words and pictures that will, should, produce the bile of shame if you are white. If you are Black, god knows what feelings such a thing invokes.

RACISM BY DEFAULT

MY NAME IS, well, call me G. (Why do you think they named it Alcoholics Anonymous?), and I'm a knee-walking, snot-flying, trembling, weepy lush. But not a practicing one. I have thirty-eight years of so-called sobriety. But I'm still not what one might call a solid upstanding citizen. I'm a poet. A writer of fiction. A biker of the motorized variety. An ex-rodeoer. I drive a Primered, chopped 1949 cruiser—it's loud. I'm not. But don't mistake quiet for passive. Digressive yes. Passive, not so much.

I'm not so good at labeling myself as I am others. Think about it. Have you thrown any labels around lately? It's become pandemic. If you're left of center it's pretty easy to talk about racist xenophobes on the right. If you're right of the middle, it can be Marxist thugs and deranged libs on the other. But the middle, it's a whole lot bigger than anyone thinks. Hell, it includes the redneck that B.H. Fairchild talks of who tried to rob a convenience store with a caulking gun, or a Dixiecrat gay whose grandfather was a KKK Grand Klagoneer or whatever they call them. I, myself, think Ike and Harry were the greatest presidents ever, aside from Lincoln. That puts me square schizoid center. I was enraged when the government killed Kennedy and that dragged me to the left. This was the abrupt end of innocence, of believing what those in power tell us. But that's a lot of other stories, as you'll see I'm fond of saying. I was pissed when the DNC sandbagged Bernie. I liked Bernie. I'd followed him for years through a Vermont newsletter titled *Seven Days* and probably know more about him than most of the people who'd have voted for him. But I digress. Aggressively. Onward.

Back in the heavy-drinking days, my (first) wife and I settled in a Midwestern city where I had accepted a job in an advertising agency. I was good at that kind of thinking and graphics that sold stuff. I got better at it, too. All the way to Los Angeles, a giant agency, and the big-money car commercials. But that's a lot of other stories.

This story is one that is painful to recount, even now, forty-plus years later. Picture cops gathered, handing out riot gear. Martin Luther King has just been assassinated and not by James Earl Ray. But that's a lot of other stories. Anyway, they had called me at home, said it was an emergency. I knew what it was about, but saw little reason to gear up. There were no riots on our side of the locks and dams of the Mississippi River, nor were there likely to be.

"Just go to where they might congregate, Look around. Take plate numbers. Be aware." "They" are, of course, Blacks. "We" were volunteers. Not wannabe cops, but, well, let me explain.

Several of us guys had horses and we kept them at a local pig farm in a nice barn with stalls and a runway. We shared clean-up and stall-mucking duties. A week per horse owner. We set up one of the guys in a farmhouse on the property as caretaker. Let's call him Lazy Dan. There were a couple of women, too, there always are with horses, but that's a lot of other stories.

We'd ride whenever we felt like it: midnight, daytime, drunk, sober. We had cookouts and social gatherings, loud music, plenty of booze, weed—this was the sixties—and what held our loose group together was horses. My kids showed locally, and it was the one thing my wife at the time and I had in common. None of us had horse trailers, but we borrowed them, and I finally bought a one-horse that got plenty of use. Lazy Dan played the guitar and had a hell of a voice: I'd get drunk and make him sing "Early Morning Rain" over and over and over.

Then things got complicated.

A guy showed up. Mil-spec haircut, cop shades, a way of talking that was cop-like. He asked if any of us would be interested in volunteering for the sheriff's patrol. They could use guys with horses for search patrols, looking for lost kids in rough country, that sort of thing. It would be as a unit of the sheriff's mounted patrol.

"Do you guys have horse trailers?" I asked.

"Oh sure," the laconic answer, toothpick rolling.

"In order to practice, we'd need to borrow one or two every now and then," I said.

"Can be arranged." Toothpick. No eyes.

"I'll talk to the guys," I said.

One thing led to another and next thing I know, I have a Wallace sticker on my bumper. I did not place it there.

During these things that led to other things we had acquired some trailers among us, so the importance of the sheriff's mounted patrol was not high. BUT we had become a part of it. The state police were our advisors. We met weekly. At one point a trooper who was giving a talk on law enforcement said, "Before we go on, is there anyone here who might not be interested in continuing to learn about law enforcement?" Pause, during which, I remember, my hands were on my knees under the school desk. We were all seated at school desks, patrolmen and mounted unit alike. I recall starting to raise my hand. Then he went on, "Because if you aren't, there are n—rs on the streets of (the city) who could fill your shoes." Hand back on knee, sweating a bit.

A few nights before, my wife and I had had a Black couple over for dinner. The guy was an advertising art director for another agency, and we had met him and his wife at an awards ceremony. We got on well, and we wanted to get to know them better. That was what you did in advertising. Socialize with the people you liked and sometimes that would be advantageous when looking to move up or acquire talent. Like any other business, I guess.

We'd had a pleasant time. Looked forward to more.

This incident I had just taken part in, given my tacit approval to by not responding in the negative, sealed something in my mind. Cowardice by any other name is still cowardice. I look back over the years and this isn't the only reaction or lack of one that I'm ashamed of. But I would not label myself a coward. Would anyone?

I didn't like the feeling. And, though a drinker, I somehow knew that a few beers and shots wouldn't erase this or ameliorate it, as it did so many things.

I went home, told my wife what had happened. We decided, well, I had to get out of this sheriff's patrol deal, that was for sure. But how? I had already ridden in the town parade on a holiday in full uniform including a .357 Magnum on my hip, my horse nervous from the people on both sides of the street. I had been called a pig by a few hippies in the crowd, a bizarro occurrence as I was more like them than what I was impersonating. But the horse guys and I had found there were certain perks to the association with the sheriff's patrol. A couple of us had already dodged a D.U.I.

or two. There was stature involved. There was a good ol' boys sort of clique-hood and I don't mind saying that it was appealing.

My out was that if you missed more than two weekly meetings in a row, you were dismissed, out, finished. We decided, okay, I'll just miss three meetings.

I missed two. I was called by the man who'd first approached us. I made excuses, said I'd had to work late. You know the ad biz, I said. He warned me about the consequences of missing another meeting. I missed it. Breathed a sigh of relief, poured in some bourbon.

He came to the house. I had bundled up the uniform, gloves with powdered lead in the knuckles, helmet, face shield, whatever I had been issued, and answered the door.

He said, "Well, I told them boys you were in advertising, and that you had lots of night hours. That you are a good addition. What I'm sayin', don't worry about it."

He left. I did attend some more meetings. At the time, I was pretty heavily involved in martial arts, to the point of competition as a green belt, even though I could have easily ranked as a brown belt and had already performed the necessary codas. This was common among competing dojos. I knew, when I competed against other green belts, that they were held back as well, just to rack up some points. It was rare that a green belt was actually a green belt in competition.

We also participated in some forms of martial arts with our state mentors. On this particular night a trooper was demonstrating stick practice. My particular form of martial arts was close to the Korean Taekwondo in that we experienced lots of contact. It was a Japanese version, Shitō-ryū, a less common form that I had just happened into, much as I had happened into the mounted patrol. At any rate, when we took or gave contact we were taught to exhale mightily before the contact occurred, with a shout I can only try to approximate as "Cheeee-oyyytz!"

A foreign sound to any who'd not heard it before, and from very deep within the diaphragm. The air is expelled explosively.

It came automatically. I practiced at the dojo two nights a week, faithfully, and on Saturdays whenever possible. I became, shall we say, immersed. Our instructor sometimes made us sit still and draw circles on watercolor paper with a brush dipped in ink. I will never forget this man. He was an artist and colorblind. He painted versions of the American flag, Jasper Johns-like, only in grays and black oil on canvas. They were quite striking.

The night we did stick practice, we learned various ways to use the baton with both hands to fend off blows, as a projected device into the gut sword-like, etc. The instructor chose me to show how to use it when someone approaches with a weapon. The details of that night are unclear, but my resentment came up in an unexpected "Cheeee-oyyytz" and the wide-eyed instructor not only lost his baton, he went to the mat, with me over him on one knee, performing a truncated and pulled punch and throat claw.

Usually, if one beats his instructor there will be extended hell to pay, but this was turned into an advantage somehow, that one of the class was a black belt (untrue) and that one should always expect the unexpected. For some reason, it cemented me as a member of the club. And it did not reflect badly on the trooper. He asked me afterward what the fuck it was that I did there, and I explained it as best I could. Ethos-wise, I was still in the same fix as regards race.

We moved away from there to another job in advertising, other horseplay, other ways to salve my conscience as a racist by default. Bringing out underprivileged kids to ride gentle horses, for one thing. But that's a hell of a long way from marching at Selma. And I still tamp down a bit of revulsion for the white guy that didn't raise his hand to be counted.

In these strange days, my friends are varied: some gay, one transgender, some Black men and women, and people of other colors, some rednecks, some libs. Some beautiful Black people in the family now. Humans all. Flawed, like me. I don't beat myself up for not being a legendary stalwart. I don't know (m)any of those. Do you? Are you one? When you're out there shouting in a crowd of like-minded folks shouting with you, that isn't what I'm talking about. What I'm talking about is raising your hand when you're the loner. I had my chance and I fucked up. Will you? Truth to power is easy in a crowd. Not so much the other way around. For instance, Liu Xiaobo, who just died in a Chinese jail. Look him up if you don't know him. Talk about legendary stalwarts and a lone voice to power. We should all have such guts and dignity.

And this: judge not lest ye be judged. We seem to do an awful lot of that these days. These strange, strange days.

REJECTIONS: BUGS ON THE WINDSHIELD

Look at Entropy's list, or NewPages', or *Review Review*'s long listing of literary journals. Then there's Duotrope, and Trish Hopkinson's many lists, and BookFox. You'll find places to submit, no problem. New journals pop up to replace those which bit the dust after a year or two. No shortage of possibilities. Most are no-fee or reasonably priced at three bucks or so. (How the hell does *Narrative* get any submissions when they charge $26 just to read your stuff?) So you cruise the websites, find journals you like, winnow it down to a few, and submit.

Four months later your email has an exciting notice. Re: submission. It's from a lit mag you really, really wanted to get into.

You learn to scan the short message with the eye of the lizard for the fly. If the word "unfortunately" is in that scan, you've been rejected, no matter what the rest of it says. Usually for reasons of "fit." This is the softer landing pad euphemism for "we don't like your stuff." Wait, maybe not. It goes on to say please submit more of your work in the future. They don't say that to everyone. Maybe.

That means something. And what means even more is when they take the time to say something like, "You've got fans here. Keep submitting. Keep writing. You made it to the final round this time and we want to see more."

That kind of rejection makes it into a file I keep labeled "Inspiration." When I'm feeling, well, rejected, I open the file and see what words of encouragement some of the good guys have jotted.

I'm old enough to remember paper rejection slips and opening the SASE to see whether they were good ones or not. Plain "sorry, we can't use it" ones were the hardest to take. Sometimes, they'd jot a personal note on the slip. Some journals still require mail-in subs, and I've found two kinds of rejection slips. A famous review sends both kinds, and I've gotten a couple of each. One kind is a quick, cold form. The other has (printed) words added to it: "We'd like to see more of your work." The latter is (almost) cause for elation.

Considering the number of pubs out there, and the fact that a large percentage of them only accept one percent to three percent of the many, many submissions they receive (think thousands) to be accepted is an indicator that you're not wasting your time. Or when a paper rejection slip has "Fine bunch of poems" written hastily in ballpoint pen, or "Great little story, but the ending was not quite there."

All I can say is when rejections are a little more than rejections, pay attention. You'll soon learn to tell the difference. There will be periods of time when you see them and think, there's another one, like bugs on a windshield on a long summer drive. Fwap. Fwap, fwap. And they're all one kind, noting the absence of fit, all using the word unfortunately.

You indulge in paranoia. You think, who did I piss off in the lit world that they're blackballing me? Or, the interns fell asleep and to make up for lost time, trashed the slush pile and told their editor bosses, all done, anything else before I knock off for the day? Then, out of the blue, one of the emails starts with "We love ..." They not only *like* that piece you thought was pretty damn good, they LOVE it. Want to publish it in their next edition. Is it still available?

Yes it is. Then comes the bizarro rejection time. YOU email THEM, the lit mags, where your piece is still hanging fire, that the piece is no longer available. A happy task. Some of them even congratulate you. Great feeling.

It will happen to you. What more can I say? Except: keep writing, keep honing, keep crafting away.

It will happen to you. You'll make it into the exalted one-three percent. Celebrate because it ain't every day. And that's the big understatement.

THE UNKNOWN WRITER

AFTER SEVEN traditionally published books, two agents, numerous editors, and three publishers (and all that took years and an immense amount of stress) you'd think I might have earned a spot on your local bookseller's shelf. Wrong. I may never get there. Not even if I spent $50,000 on a U.S. book tour and glad-handed ten thousand customers, and signed books until I was carpally numb. It would still be "Who?"

I'm not complaining (whining maybe, but with a sort of smile). I get it. I'm even getting a sixth, and maybe a seventh, book published this year, by the same publisher as some of my others. And I'm half done with another book, a thriller to which even I don't know the ending.

I paid my dues. I sat in conference rooms in L.A. with well-dressed men who flipped through my treatments and my screenplays and declared them quite good, but ... Lots of buts. But that's been done. But that's not what the public wants. But noir is over with. But there are too many laughs for noir.

One of them said, "Here's an idea that'll write itself." It didn't. I balanced a pencil on a sheet of blank paper and waited. I said to the man, "It's not doing it."

"Not doing what?"

The pencil fell over.

"Writing itself."

"This meeting is over."

I sent manuscript after manuscript to agent after agent. A legendary New York agent even contacted *me* after reading a short story of mine. He asked if I had a novel. *Do I ever*, I thought, and sent him one. He said, "Well, it's not exactly a right fit, can you do another one?"

An agent was interested in a screenplay I did, but wanted me to change the opening scenes. I said fine. The agent passed away. That screenplay was done on a typewriter—that's how long ago *that* was.

Dues. I wrote short stories for lit reviews. Lots of them. So far, I've been in over eighty of those literary journals with all different short stories, poetry, and essays. I won some writing contests. My first book was the result of a win. A university publisher and enough money to fix the soffits. I thought I was on the way. Amazon sells the book for fifteen dollars. They pay me six dollars and seventy-five cents per book. I buy the book for seven dollars and fifty cents from the university publisher. Dumbass business model, is it not?

There's a variation of the question, "If you're so smart, why ain't you rich?" It goes, "If you're such a hot writer, why ain't you famous?" I can earnestly answer, "Beats me." It's not like I haven't tried. So here's the deal: I did most of that writing for the sheer accomplishment of it. I'd say joy of it, but that's not quite right. There was damn little joy involved.

I guess I write because I have to. If it resonates with a public out there, fine. If it doesn't, I'm not going to try and figure out what does. Joyce Carol Oates didn't determine what struck a chord with a great number of people and then write that melody over and over. She just wrote her ass off and still does. She got known. I'm betting she writes what makes her feel good. Or just *feel*. And a lot of people happen to love it. I'm betting Joan Didion didn't run her words through focus groups. And so on.

So, it's settled. I'll keep writing. And it'll be for me ... then, hopefully, for those readers who are in that slipstream of words and feeling that speaks to them a little bit, that pulls on them. Wow, that's gravy, as an old adman I knew and admired used to say.

I'll close for now with this. It's an email I sent to a friend who read my latest book and who left a nice review for it. And it's from my heart:

(Subject: Thanks times five)

(1) Thanks for having the interest to get Ruined Days (2) Thanks for taking the time and effort to buy it (3) Very importantly, thanks for reading it (4) thanks ever so much for taking the time and effort to submit a reader review, and (5) thanks for the well-worded and considerate review that will help others make their decision. There are a lot of steps to help an unknown sell a book he believes in, and they come well after the years of the writer's life invested in that book. You took 'em, and I want you to know how appreciated it is. G.

THEY'RE STILL STEALING VAN GOGHS

WHILE RESEARCHING Nazi art thefts for a novel, *L.A. Hardscape*, I was brought up short by the audacity and sheer scope of the crime. I had seen *The Monuments Men*, but that had seemed like an entertainment, an embellished tale based on fact, and it didn't really dilate my cortex like the tons of print that you can dig up on the thefts and I just scratched the surface. Hermann Goering's "collection" alone amounted to almost 2,000 works of art when you count sculpture and tapestries along with the 1,400 paintings. And, like a true obsessive bureaucrat, he and his minions cataloged every single one. Including whom they stole it from. These guys were nothing if not methodical. And it should be mentioned here that the entire amount of stolen art and artifacts is much greater than what adorned the walls of Carinhall, Göring's chalet. The Third Reich's amassment of looted objects was in the hundreds of thousands and storage in salt mines, caves, warehouses, and tunnels from 1933 to the end of the war are legend. A lifetime could be spent researching the thefts. Göring's collection alone has taken researchers years to trace. Efforts are ongoing.

I found myself looking up painting after painting and, being an artist myself, sighing over each and every one. This guy surrounded himself with beauty and splendor, the best of the best—I don't know what the metaphor is here; this truly pernicious rat bastard making his grand chateau outside Berlin, Carinhall, the depository of the world's art genius. All of it looted. There is no metaphor, so I won't struggle for one. Hitler's number two man was one hell of a collector, emphasis on hell.

I was wasting a lot of time looking at great paintings (Can that be time wasted? If you're trying to get a novel done, I suppose it could be), many of which I'd glimpsed in art history courses in art school. My eyes were glazing over. Just one of these paintings could set me up in fast cars and tall cotton for the rest of my life.

At this point I was eyeing van Gogh's *Bridge at Langlois in Arles*. And that's when I made the decision to follow the Nazi trail of theft through one artist, thus paring down the time spent and making the task less gargantuan. I looked up this painting and found that the bridge at Arles was the subject of four van Gogh oil paintings, some watercolors and a series of drawings. All of these are just as superb as you would think. He was about thirty-five when he produced them in 1888 in Arles, France, where he lived at the time and where he enjoyed the height of his career and productivity. In less than fifteen months, he produced more than 200 paintings.

The bridge reminded him of his homeland, the Netherlands, and he sent a framed version of it to an art dealer there. One of the 1888 versions was taken by Göring and it was one of his favorites. He stole van Gogh's *Portrait of Dr. Gachet* as well but ended up selling it in 1937. But not the bridge. That stayed at Carinhall. But where is it now?

I lost the trail at Carinhall, though a book might provide some clues.

A 518-page book, *Beyond the Dreams of Avarice: The Hermann Goering Collection*, published in 2009, could possibly shed some light on which bridge painting was in that collection, and also provide a trail of provenance, which in many cases is labyrinthine. The only information I could find on van Gogh's *Portrait of Dr. Gachet* was that it reportedly had been sold. To who was not divulged. But another, third, *Portrait of Dr. Gachet*—of which only two were known—showed up in Greece in the inheritance of a struggling author, Doreta Peppa. It had been "liberated" by her late father in a Resistance attack on a Nazi train. They'd been after ammunition, but Peppa's father also made off with a crate of paintings. One of the paintings was the van Gogh, and other items included a notebook of his drawings. Nazi stamps on the backs of the items were validated as official, and the items themselves appear to be indisputably authentic. Why isn't Doreta rich? No one will touch the art, possibly because it may cast doubt on the authenticity of other van Gogh paintings now hanging in galleries and private collections. It's a Byzantine story but suffice it to say she may be the richest poor struggling author in the history of literature and, by way of the Nazis, the art world. She remains penniless, and the art is in a temperature-controlled vault which further drains her meager income.

The art trove is hers, having been traced as far back as possible, and no one has come forward to claim the pieces. Not the family from which they were stolen or anyone else. It's quite possible the previous owners were the last of a family line and met their end at the hands of the Nazis. The crateful never reached its intended destination, where it would no doubt have been punctiliously cataloged.

The notebook alone is probably worth $3.5 million, and a respected authority said he believes it to be van Gogh's student workbook from the Royal Academy of Fine Art in Brussels. The age and the paper have been confirmed in separate tests. Other tests and samplings have further corroborated the pieces as genuine. The van Gogh Museum offered to authenticate the Gachet painting, but a contract they sent stated they would keep it forever. For free. Meanwhile Ms. Peppa has lost her home due to search, storage, and authentication costs. The Nazis, it appears, have left their mark, and curse, on van Gogh and the world's fine-art market once again.

The total estimated worth of her crate of stolen Nazi art, which includes a Cezanne nude, is over $100 million. Conspiracy theorists are blaming a bullying art cartel for refusing to legitimize the find until they can get their hands on it some other way. I don't know who is to blame in such a bizarre situation, but it does irk me that the art isn't shared with the world. Isn't that the point of great art? It's almost a sure thing that the art is real—none of the tests would seem to indicate otherwise. Which begs the question: WTF?

Anyway, the trail ran cold on Nazi-looted van Goghs. But mysteries abound, and who doesn't love those? Especially mystery writers (literature seems to be intertwined in this stolen art business). Bestseller Lynne Kennedy (*The Triangle Murders, Time Exposure, Pure Lies*) came upon just such a mystery while researching *Deadly Provenance*, a novel of deception involving a Nazi-looted van Gogh oil titled *Still Life: Vase with Oleanders*. Who better to pursue it? The Brooklyn-born author worked with the San Diego Sheriff's Department and SDPD Crime Lab in forming forensic studies for teachers and students. In adding authenticity to her books, she worked with museum and historical experts as well as crime-solving officials at a time when the *CSI* TV shows were becoming popular. Great credentials for investigating a lost van Gogh. While she solved the case in her novel, the painting remains missing in real life, and Kennedy herself is still on the case. If anyone has any leads they are encouraged to contact her; a good start is her website, Lynne Kennedy Mysteries. There, you'll find fascinating links to interviews and progress notes.

The painting, also known as *Vase of Irises Against a Yellow Background*, was one of thirty or so that had been at the Bernheim-Jeune Gallery in Paris. Suspecting an imminent Nazi raid in 1940, the owners packed them off to Château de Rastignac near Bordeaux. In 1941, the Nazis tracked them there, looted as much as they could, and burned the chateau to the ground. The paintings, including the van Gogh, have not been seen since. And Lynne Kennedy has unearthed some very interesting information in her search, having contacted people and museums who are close to the source.

Nazis weren't the only thieves interested in van Gogh paintings. Two of his paintings were stolen in 2002 from the van Gogh Museum in Amsterdam, a seascape and a painting of a church in Neunen where his father had been pastor. The burglars climbed to the roof using a ladder, broke through a window, and exited out the side of the building using a rope. The theft seems like the stuff of movies. During an investigation of the Camorra Mafia family in Italy, the oils were recovered in 2016.

At the time of the crime, the paintings were worth about $4.5 million. Works by van Gogh have sold for up to $82.5 million at auction, but the stolen works were from his Hague period and of a style that sells for a good deal less.

Another vase-and-flowers van Gogh oil, *Poppy Flowers*, was stolen in 2010 from Mohamed Mahmoud Khalil Museum in Cairo. Its value is around $50 million and one can imagine a white-suited, red-fezzed Sydney Greenstreet bargaining with Humphrey Bogart for its return. Egyptian officials believed they had caught the perps of the painting pilferage, arresting two Italian suspects attempting to board a plane at Cairo International Airport. No deal. It's still among the missing van Goghs. It had been stolen previously in 1977 from the same museum and recovered ten years later in Kuwait. If you see a small painting of a bunch of yellow flowers and a couple of red ones in a vase, give the museum a call.

If you have a van Gogh or two, you might want to beef up your ADT alarm system with some of those impenetrable laser-lined security mazes that only George Clooney could negotiate. Or was that Cary Grant? In one of my books, *Ruined Days*, a New Orleans art gallery uses holographic images for its most expensive sculptures. A Degas ballerina revolves under a light, for all intents and purposes a solid bronze figurine, until someone reaches for it and touches only air. As the gallery owner explains to the main character in the story, "Some collectors prefer to have the original in a vault somewhere. We make these up for them so they can appreciate the piece with no reservations about it being damaged or stolen."

Perhaps in the future, van Goghs, Titians, Klimts, and Caravaggios will be exquisitely projected images. Once the lights go out in the museum or gallery, so do the paintings. You're still in the presence of genius, once removed. And you're not supposed to touch the works anyway. Sort of like zoos of the future: holographic images, and if your kid jumps into the gorilla cage they won't have to shoot anything. That, to me, is preferable to jailed animals. But hey, that's me.

Back to van Gogh, Nazi loot, and paintings of questionable authenticity that continue to surface. This one, signed Vincent, was purchased for a few hundred guilders in the Dutch city of Breda around the time WWII began. A still life featuring an open Bible, clay pipe, and some other items, such as a bottle and a drape of some kind behind; it is primarily monochromatic with yellow ochres and greens. The owners, Catherine and Malcolm Head from Guildford, believe it to have been painted at the parsonage in Neunen, where van Gogh lived between 1883 and 1885. They've spent a great deal of money on age testing and other samplings which do corroborate the time, if not the artist. But the van Gogh Museum dismisses the painting as a fake, citing stylistic differences.

They stated that it is more likely the oil was by the lesser-known female Dutch artist, Wilhelmina Vincent. Hence the signing "Vincent" in the lower corner. Although, to me, it looks like van Gogh's signature style, but it is slanted uphill. As art restorer Robert Mitchell says, "It could well be a genuine painting by Vincent van Gogh but everyone in the art world will say no before they say yes." That one's been around since 1997 and shows no sign of conclusion.

In the "You just never know" department, van Gogh's *Portrait of Doctor Felix Rey*, which now hangs in the Pushkin Museum of Fine Arts, Russia has an interesting backstory. It was once used to plug a hole in a chicken coop. Dr. Rey worked on van Gogh after the legendary ear incident, and to show his gratitude, van Gogh painted his portrait. Rey never liked it much, as evidenced by its disposition as chicken house insulation. I wonder if whoever found that painting had any problem making people believe it was genuine. "I was tearing down an old chicken coop and there was a van Gogh on the wall inside. Yeah, I think it's real, don't you?"

While the van Gogh Museum often declines to accept surfacing paintings as authentic, they do, through diligent research, welcome the ones they deem worthy. *Sunset at Montmajour* is such a painting, and it's not even signed. Inventoried in the collection of Theo van Gogh, it was sold in 1901. No record of it existed until a Norwegian industrialist bought it and displayed it in his home. Advised that it was not a van Gogh, he stored it in the attic. In the 1990s the van Gogh Museum dismissed it because it was unsigned. "Hey, not so fast," someone said. In 2011, they started a two-year investigation. Exhaustive tests and a letter of provenance from Vincent to Theo resulted in a 2013 unveiling and hanging of the oil in the museum.

Meanwhile, they're still plotting thefts out there. And fakery abounds. But I just saw one on eBay. "Vincent van Gogh Painting. Bearing 'VINCENT' Signature at bottom left. This piece appears to be in decent good condition and will be sold 'as is.'" Hmm, where's the phone number of the van Gogh Museum? This might be the break I've been looking for.

VISUALIZING: NOT A WOO-WOO SCIENCE

I WAS IN Los Angeles, working at an ad agency, a big one. It was a quieter time, pre 9/11, pre all the vitriolic spewing back and forth about politics, pre worst fires in California history, pre meltdowns of everything. I was attending focus groups for automobile advertising, and marveling at how groups would show up for cookies and a couple of bucks and then sit and talk about their dogs for the session. What about trouble-free operation? More power? Comfort approaching luxury? Frustrated session leaders tried to keep them on subject, but little was gleaned unless one read between their answers.

I slid out of one such group midway through a digression about wines thinking *gag me with a sun-dried tomato,* and on the way home pulled into a tack store in Torrance. I'd passed it before, and noticed rodeo posters in the window. I'd owned horses, had rodeoed in Kansas, Missouri, and Texas, rough stock, and missed the adrenaline-producing wildness of it, the sounds and bustle of the chutes, the preparation. As I entered the store, the smell of new leather, liniments, and bagged feed took me back and a genuine lump-in-the-throat nostalgia set in. I touched some saddles, wandered to a wall showing framed pictures of rodeo events, and was struck by one straight-backed fellow, balance hand in the air, on a twisting bull.

"That's Ivan," a female voice said. "He's sixty-nine on that bull."

Sixty-nine, I thought. *I've got thirty years on that guy.* I could get back in the game. Do it right this time.

"Does he compete much?"

"All the time," she answered. "Mainly Old Timer rodeos, when his arthritis allows. He's in great shape for his age."

Her admiration was evident. I glanced at her. Jeans tucked into western boots buckaroo-style, denim shirt, big rodeo-queen buckle. She looked like Kansas, in the best possible way: sunburnt face, sun-streaked hair in a ponytail. Maybe twenty.

"Can I help you find anything?"

My lost youth, I thought. *You could help there. A lot.* "No, thanks, just looking right now. You carry bull ropes? Cow bells?"

She walked to another area, picked up a cow bell, and clanked it at me. Just that sound gave me a small rush. We both laughed.

"Best and loudest," she said, clanking it again.

On the drive up the hill to Palos Verdes, I knew what was to come. I had bought two videos at the tack store of best bull rides. This was before PBR, Professional Bull Riders, which you can stream now. Streaming wasn't an option. Video tapes preceded DVDs.

I had just read an article on visualizing. What I took away was the fact that two sets of basketball players practiced free throws and then competed against one another. One group had practiced by doing. The other group by merely visualizing the act. The visualizers beat the doers. There was more to the test but that's basically what happened.

I was in great shape. I ate fish a couple times a week, lots of fruits and vegetables, few sweets, no soda, I smoked but didn't drink. I worked out daily. So part of my regimen was set. The other was to watch the two videos every night to see what the best rides had that I hadn't done years before. I'd carried a PRCA permit, but I had never earned a card. Professional Rodeo Cowboys Association required you to win a certain amount of money in a year, and I never had. I'd placed well in some non-PRCA jackpot rodeos but hadn't really examined why those rides were more successful than others. That was back in my drinking days, however, and I wasn't one prone to a lot of introspection.

   Watching the videos showed me that balance was the main reason these cowboys were winning. They weren't trying to muscle their way; that's folly with a bull. Balance and going with a spin, not fighting it, the balance arm flinging back and forth like a windshield wiper, helps the rider back down on his hand, no air between him and the bull. Once there's air between your butt and the bull, only luck will bring you back on your hand—that, or a herculean strength-sapping effort. Once you're airborne you'd better unwrap that hand and get free. The alternative is to be a rag doll attached by your arm to a big, agile thing that wants your ass.

   This is one reason I never did the "suicide wrap" but always left a bubble of rope above my hand so I could get free when I needed to deplane.

   There was no Google back then so I couldn't put together a string of SEO words to find what I wanted. Had I been able, it would have been bull riding champion visualization psycho-cybernetics Southern California. It would have brought me Gary Leffew. As it happened, I researched all of that and more, and it came up Gary Leffew, Santa Maria, California.

Had I known I was doing all this prep for the first bull I would ride since my rodeo days and that it would be my absolute last bull ever, I may not have undertaken the adventure. But I didn't know anything of the kind. I was in the kind of shape that makes one feel indestructible. Look at Ivan, now seventy, still riding. I looked up Old Timers Rodeo Association, saw several California venues. Weekends I could ride bulls. Weekdays, write automobile commercials. Heck, I could even enter some PRCA events, maybe earn a card this time.

I re-read *Psycho-Cybernetics* by Maxwell Maltz. I'd read it years before, and now, of all people, Gary Leffew had recommended it for rodeoers. I felt connected to some universal truths, actually did, and actually was at that time. I was into the Tao of bull riding, bingeing on hours of videotape every single night and thinking about it every day. I padded my weight bench with blankets and luggage and practiced sitting on my tied hand, balance hand anticipating every switch of direction. I still had my glove and spurs from Donny Gay's school in Mesquite, Texas, and a new rope from the tack shop, rosined and ready. I'd saved my chaps, my hat. My glove was soft and supple with mink oil, my rope stretched and worked.

You may be thinking that there's got to be a gargantuan difference between sitting on a bunch of blankets and luggage on a bench press and on an actual fire-breathing, snot-flying bull, and, of course, you're right. But visualization and realistic imagination were compensating for all that. I had rodeoed before, enough to know what that moment was like, the quick nod, the arm on the gate, the gate swinging open and the bull rocketing out. I had done that, plenty. But never as prepared as I now was. Somehow I knew like never before the racket, the smell, the sweat, the commotion of it. I was there.

A word about bucking machines. They're no good for preparing for bulls. They swing around and pitch front and back, but in no way do they emulate what a bull does. No effing way.

I don't recall the drive to Santa Maria. I'd taken a vacation for this. I do recall arriving. And the first meeting with Gary Leffew, a bull-riding legend. He asked the small group if we'd read *Psycho-Cybernetics* as he had suggested when we'd signed up. A couple of us mumbled in the affirmative. Some of the younger cowboys looked away or into a middle distance, wanting to get on with it. There was no quiz, no recrimination, just a look at us—a beat longer than usual. Maybe a half-smile. Then, down to business. Forms and waivers had been signed, questions answered. That's all a jumble in my mind. What I recall more vividly is the bull. The chute. The handler fishing my rope through with a rod and the rope end handing it to me to complete the circuit around the bull's girth and my hand. It had been several years, but it came back instantly. I wrapped my gloved hand tight to the bull, pounded my hand a couple of times, left a large bubble of rope to pull when the time came. The bull was a black Brangus, calm and almost soporific in the chute. I kept my boots away from his sides and the gate, my left arm resting on the gate top. I nodded. The gate swung open and out he came, bucking twice, then spinning left. I felt the vortex but kept myself from going "into the well" by pulling down on my gloved hand, gripping with my spurs. Then he switched direction, and I stayed with him, balance hand waving and helping.

I felt good. The arena was a whirl, but I knew I had him and he was a good ride, an agile bull. Then, pop! I heard the sound, or think I did. Like an air rifle. And I was airborne. I unwrapped the rope, sailed, and rolled, back up to my feet.

I never forgot the quick critique from Leffew.

"What happened? You had him. You were doing great ..."

I held my right arm in to my side, and the trainer approached. He asked me a couple of questions, kneaded my arm with practiced fingers, then conferred with Leffew.

They came back. It was decided I should drive to the nearest ER and get an x-ray. It looked like school was out for me. When I asked what it might be, the trainer said he thought it was ligaments and would require surgery. It was and did. Tommy John surgery in L.A. by the same sports doctors who attended to the Raiders and John himself.

But visualization had worked. *Psycho-Cybernetics* had worked. If it worked for bull riding, what else could it accomplish? I had ridden a very good athletic bull better than I had ever ridden before. I was *with* him, and he was trying to throw me every way he could pull from his agility trick book and I was a microsecond ahead of him. Then frailty hit. My ligaments couldn't quite take it.

I was equal parts disappointed and animated. I would have won the go-round on the best bull of the day.

After I healed up I went home to Kansas, found some acres and a one-hundred-year-old farmhouse. I had horses again, married, and life took other turns. The reason I sat down and wrote this was *visualization*. There are things I want and one of them is to finish a novel that I let languish. Any writer knows how tough that is, getting a re-ride on that bull. After five books, you'd think I wouldn't let a sixth get the best of me, but this time it'll take more than showing up. I plan to visualize this one. As soon as I'm finished with this piece.

WELTERWEIGHTS

SEARCHING FOR a watchable program, any damn thing, while I ate a sensible meal of turkey, broccoli, and sliced carrots, I came upon the start of a welterweight bout. At first, when I saw the tattoos and the floor signs, the jumble of advertising, I thought, *Oh man, one of those godawful mixed martial arts things*, but saw "Boxing" in the description, so I stayed put.

Boxing still has a positional sanctification to me. That's the first of three sanctifying acts in which the subjects are set apart, if not yet "saved." Professional boxing, I now know, has few participants who undergo the tripartite, the triple whammy of grace. Survival of brain, body, and achievement beyond the ring. Sugar Ray Robinson made it. George Foreman. Tyson, in his way.

Back to the first part of the three-part deal. I'm not getting all cathedra on you here, or churchy and thurible-swinging, although some of that is analogous to pugilism. I use positional sanctification in my interpretation of its literal sense: set apart and in line for greater glory. These welterweights had flat earned their places in PS. They were fighting for more now.

At this point in their careers, both had won their last six fights. Six in a row. That's big in a savage game like boxing, and it brought me closer to the edge of my seat as I ate; it meant a must-win mentality was a force here. They each had to prove they were, yeah, champ, even if it wasn't a championship fight. Their trajectory was an eventual championship bout. The winner would have the momentum to get there quicker. It was their time, high time they met. I was rapt and my food cooled, neglected on the coffee table.

It must not have been the big event on the card; the crowd seemed sparse to me. When introduced, in that wonderful stentorian ring-strutting theatricality of the announcer, both Krael and Bone got roughly the same amount of light applause and whistling. Both danced and skipped in acknowledgement, appreciation, faces a bit distorted by mouth guards, causing a grinning sort of rictus. They were ready, nerves as evident as their fitness.

The blue-gloved ref showed them both where he judged the beltline to be. Krael's red boxing trunks were long, like Bone's black trunks, but they had rows of shimmering gold fringe, similar to a shimmy dancer's in the era of Gatsby. Showy and kind of fun. But they somehow furthered the impression of *Danger, here. Don't be fooled.*

I won't go round by round. Some very good, tight boxing ensued. Both Cameron Krael and Erick Bone are graceful, aggressive fighters. Bone is twenty-nine, Krael twenty-four. When my wife got home from work, she grimaced a bit at what I was watching. She likes to relax with something lighter. I said, "As soon as this is over, I'll watch anything you want, but this is sort of special."

"Special?"

"Yes," I said. "I don't know what kind of guys these are, but I do know they are endowed with more guts than is usually handed out in that department." She watched some, remarking on Krael's outfit. Then she began to appreciate the rhythm, the back and forth, the ... boxing. But she didn't like it.

I used to enjoy boxing. As a child, I recall listening to matches on a big, polished wood Zenith radio with my grandfather explaining what was going on. Uppercut. Cross. Body punches. My uncle was a boxer. He showed me how to follow through on a punch, shoulder into it. "Don't peck away on your opponent, reduce his fight." I tried it out at the Salvation Army Gym, Downtown KC, with one of my best friends, a good boxer who went on to Golden Gloves and amateur status. It didn't take with me. I couldn't use the fear to my advantage. The pain. Later on, in other sports I could, but I just couldn't get primal at that age, that time in my accumulation of whatever moxie I tried for or pretended to have. The ones who do, though—they have my admiration and my awe. Krael and Bone have it in spades.

Krael took some shots from the older fighter and was stunned momentarily, but he gave some of the same back before that round ended. By the tenth round, it looked so even, you really didn't know how it would score. The expert judges wouldn't have an easy time. Bone had been stunned as well, but perhaps not to the extent of Krael's quick flounder and comeback.

The blows to the heads of each were the focal point for me. I found them hard to watch, hard not to. The explosive spray of sweat, the concussions, the jarring effect. In cold, clinical terms, I kept gauging what the neurodegenerative consequences might be. How long can a man do this? That was never a consideration years ago, for most of us who watched boxing. It is now. Awareness. I was so happily unaware. The fighters were like characters in a movie—they went down, reappeared in other movies. Now they are so, so real.

The decision was close. Bone won. The last six fights, wins for each, now seven for Bone. Krael will win again, but must start a new streak.

I will watch these young men again, with other opponents, and I will pull for them.

But I won't enjoy it.

WHY I WRITE

"Poesy, man. *The world is full of it. It's beautiful and crazy and sometimes violent, sometimes peace-inducing. In every language. I had to join in. The overall song sucked me into it. You know the feeling. To hear Dylan Thomas in his own voice utter those head-shakingly gorgeous combinations of words and meanings. Whoa. Do I aspire to that exaltation? Heck yeah, why not? Do I hold a candle to it? No, but I'm trying. It's like rodeo, man. You're out there with your try in the arena, big or small, for a public to look at, laugh at, cheer, jeer."*

That's an excerpt from my foreword from *Scattered Cranes*, a poetry collection (Pski's Porch Publishing, 2017) and it says why I write as well as anything. There are so many reasons. Why do I weld steel sculptures? Why did I drag race in high school? Why did I rodeo? Why did I attend a Robert Frost lecture by myself when I was a kid? Why did I write poetry in art school?

It's a yearning. If you listen to the blues, the real thing, you can hear it. You just close your eyes and lean back into it. Pure jazz, the kind that Ahmad Jamal and MJQ came up with years ago when it was called "modern," explains the yearning and so does gut-bucket country with a fine-ass groove. Well, none of it may *explain* the yearning, but it has a fix on it; it "gets it." It's why they do it. The expression of something within that just has to come out. *Has* to.

When I was a kid, I got a little printing press. It had rubber type you could set and make words with. I was the first fake news, before some journalism as we know it today; I made up stories about neighbors and people at the grocery store. "Leaks" attributable to anonymous sources. Scandalous stuff about Russian espionage and odd goings-on in the dark of night. I didn't know it, but I was writing fiction, economical fiction because it was a bitch setting words, so I made them short and to the point. When you're a typesetter/reporter/author, you don't digress a lot.

But I was hooked, and I read the books my folks left lying around. Paperbacks like *Tobacco Road* and those written by Mickey Spillane. Crime thrillers. Novels by Pearl S. Buck and Edna Ferber. While I didn't understand some of the words, I was transported. Some words sent me to the dictionary. Words did that. Didion does that today, and I love her for it. Twenty, thirty times a book.

Words.

I look at the words I'm writing now and think that maybe, just maybe, someone might like them. These words might affect someone. And I'm a little closer to solving the mystery of why I write.

I once expressed awe at an eighty-year-old woman who went elk hunting in the winter. The man I was talking to said, "I guess nobody told her she couldn't."

And that's as good a reason as any.

WRITING WOMEN: HOW I DO IT

I WAS BROUGHT up around non-doormat women. Some were flinty and chopped chickens' heads off at a backdoor stump, some were humorous but watch out if you got their Irish up, some would clean just-caught fish unflinchingly, throwing the guts to waiting cats, and others said *Nope, I don't do fish or windows*, and poured another martini. They were all deeply human and met tribulation head-on. They knew no other way. They all had that thing called *character*. One grandmother was from Little Dixie in Missouri and her ancestors fought in the Revolutionary War. The other was destined to be an opera singer, but she opted for the ranch life in Grants Pass, Oregon. And I had a step-grandmother from London who was married to an Episcopal minister, aunts who had married but ended up single, a mother who stepped off a cruise liner in Curaçao and refused to reboard until demands were met. She didn't back off from cancer late in life, and she damn near held that off.

So, when I write women, they're informed by these and others I've met over the years. Some are strong, some aren't, but they all have my respect. I don't think I write any cardboard cutouts or "typicals." I'd like to think they all have dimension, the spark of humanity, something that gives them a bit of a lift off the page in the readers' eyes. I hope to do the same for men, of course. In a novel I'm writing, a connected sort, a bad guy, shows my protagonist a surprising side by serving at a St. Joseph's Table shelter in Wilmington Harbor, Los Angeles. And he mops afterward. And his wife—whom Hunter, my protagonist meets for the first time—is a cigarette-smoking, wisecracking fun lady who makes him laugh and brings him out of his funk. He has to rethink black and white, either/or, good and bad.

He, himself, is not a complete stalwart. He quit boxing due to the aforementioned bad guy and his own somewhat rigid principles, but temptations circle him like creatures around a night campfire. There's even a bit of woo-woo in what could be hallucinatory episodes, perhaps caused by a fighter's neurodegeneration ... or not.

Without giving away too much, the main women in the book tend toward a healthy self-respect and a no-pushover bias. One was a victim of a relationship so toxic, she stole an axe handle at Home Depot and ruined the day of her restraining-order-ignoring ex with it. She ends up working with the protagonist, Hunter, on a loose sort of work-release program instigated by an LAPD cop friend of the boxer turned PI. She is a punkish skater whose computer skills are so far off the charts I almost wrote her out of the story. I didn't want to trespass on *Dragon Tattoo* territory, but I had to wonder where she came from if not that. Nor did I want her quirky and goth as on *CSI* and other TV investigative tropes.

I traced her back to the nascent gleam in my MacBook notes and saw she was a Florida urchin, as was her boyfriend, that they had come to Los Angeles to do the stars-in-the-eyes thing. Then it went to homeless bad, and poor choices led to penny-ante drug use/peddling. It got real in a hurry when her boyfriend tried to turn her out.

As I wrote her (Dixie, originally Winnie, conceived in a Winn-Dixie meat cold room) abandoned by her Appalachian mother, then a runaway, but ambitious. She gets some good counseling on her journey and early successes in a User Experience (UX) lab setting, and she's off and running. The backstory is barely a part of the novel, but I recall that much and a bit of it comes out during the story. As she takes form on the pages, she's wary, scruffy, but pretty in a punk sort of appearance, and highly intelligent. She also has a great sense of humor, which I find attractive in female leads. The latter two traits mesh well with Hunter's IQ and humor, while also causing some stress.

While writing these people, I carefully have to weigh their credibility to the reader. I want to remain somewhat realistic and not get into the "rollicking noir" antics game. Some writers are adept at that and do it well. I have a hard time carrying it off in anything longer than a short-short story. This can't be Nick and Nora, however wonderfully Dashiell Hammett wrote them into a life of their own. (You're saying, "I see what you did there, putting yourself in high company ..." Hey, we all aspire.) And there's a dog, an aging Australian Shepherd named Walden that Hunter met on a landscaping job in Manhattan Beach. Walden, Hunter, and Dixie become partners.

Dixie has flaws. She can be intransigent, jealous, petty, foul-mouthed. She's a rough diamond, but a gem nevertheless. Other women in the story include Karla and Canaday. Karla is a powerful fifty-ish beauty, enigmatic, crafty yet on the verge of motherly. Canaday is a sharp advertising agency producer and a friend of Hunter's. She's sexy, sharp-tongued, and tends to bring out Dixie's green-eyed side.

They clash. And there's Murph's wife. Murph is Hunter's Palos Verdes landlord, and Pat, his wife, is a sensible lady, affable but easily soured by weather, bills, and circumstances. She resents Murph letting Hunter slide on the rent in exchange for landscaping and gardening chores.

There's a much larger story in *L.A. Hardscape*, but it's either in the book or on the way to it. Hunter and Dixie are working in Santa Barbara on a massive landscaping project that involves ... well, the book—it'll all be in the book. Oh, Hunter is in possession of a possibly stolen Giacometti bronze which he's hidden in a fertilizer bag. And he may have killed a mob torpedo. But I've said too much. This is about writing women. And dogs, and bad guys, and rusted-out classic Porsches with rakes sticking out of them, and shadowy men in black from Kansas City, and human trafficking, and ... like that. It may end up in a drawer, but I hope not. The women are too strong to stay there for long in any case.

THE COUNSELOR. WHO SAYS EVIL IS BANAL?

AHH, SOMETHING I can sink my teeth into. Cormac McCarthy's mind-bendingly brilliant screenplay. There used to be an account executive at the ad agency where I spent fifteen or twenty years at the end of my career, who would look at a campaign or single promotional effort prepared by my team, and say. "I don't get it." Fortunately she was overruled by those who did get it because they got it easily. She was hired because of an MBA, probably. She learned answers to tests and probably said "I don't get it" to the professors every so often.

The point(s). I'm getting to that. I was rather surprised by the reaction to *The Counselor*. Many said, "No plot." They are woefully mistaken. Many said, "Too many loose ends to attend to mentally." They are the lazy ones, the ones who want to be fed the usual: some nudity, violence, and cars blowing up. All I can say to them is, "Thanks for your input." Hrh hrh hrh. And then there were those who didn't "get it." Oh, boy. I don't know what to say to them. Maybe what I said to the account executive, "How exquisitely sad."

Now to the meat. Cormac McCarthy never wrote anything that wasn't stupendous. Some books left me bummed and my eyes glazed, but they also wowed the shit outta me with The Writing. From *The Orchard Keeper* on. His *Blood Meridian* was the most powerfully poetic, beautifully written apocalyptic violence I have ever read. A classic, often compared to Faulkner's *As I Lay Dying*, and named to the twenty-five best novels ever written. Many more beautiful books followed.

So, "No plot," "Too much going on," and "I don't get it," don't signify. They just don't. Sweep them aside.

I first saw the paperback screenplay on Amazon and passed it up, though I had a McCarthy jones that never goes away. I know the format and didn't want to read him that way. Big mistake. I saw the film on DVD and had to replay the soliloquies for their dazzling beauty and philosophical pith. Then I sent for the screenplay. I read it oh, so slowly, savoring the descriptions, the dialogue, the metaphors, the lurking meanings in the shadows.

A word about evil. The screenplay is like reading some Apocryphal forbidden church document. Evil is a character in *The Counselor*. Somewhere along the road (pardon that), McCarthy has run into evil. This is not to say he is, but he dealt with it along the way, either absorbed it or rejected it. But he knows *It*. My fancy is that there was some sort of crossroads before his first literary efforts, and he came away with extraordinary powers, like Robert Johnson, the king of the Delta blues, another Faustian legend. Reading this screenplay is a goosebump trip.

"... anything you can say about a diamond is in the nature of a flaw."

There's an instructive passage between the counselor and

a diamond merchant early in the script, in which a large, impressive diamond is viewed from the underside and seen to be cut in a way that doesn't allow the crown and pavilion to be aligned. "Once the first facet is cut," says the dealer, "there is no going back." He also says that the forms of our undertakings are complete at their beginnings. The counselor has already set his in motion by the time he buys his beloved Laura (Penélope Cruz) the spectacular engagement stone.

In one telling sentence, the dealer says, "We are not looking for merit. This is a cynical business. We seek only imperfection." Something the prince of darkness might say, but the diamond dealer is not evil; he is merely stating fact, subtly advancing the story forward.

Many such instances occur.

Cameron Diaz's character, Malkina, is insatiably evil. She escalates because evil is her drug, and she's totally addicted. She pumps Laura for information on how to initiate the telling of confession to a priest. When she does enter the confessional, what follows is truly unsettling. She may want to be forgiven for her sins, but she also wants to tell them to the priest, trophy depravities. She wants to sense his horror. She's also beautiful, but in a very hard-edged way, like a diamond. One that is not quite aligned when seen from certain angles.

The casting in this film is marvelous, direction superb. Perfection throughout, bit part to major. Javier Bardem must be an actor's actor. His role as Reiner, an increasingly reckless, though troubled, voluptuary is breathtaking. All the actors enjoy and "get" Cormac McCarthy's words and impetus to a T.

The counselor naively decides to get in and out of a very dirty business, fast money to sufflate his investment exponentially—but the filth is a tar baby. A hit-you-on-the-head metaphor for the whole business is the transportation device for the drugs. They are sealed in fifty-gallon drums, then hidden in a septic-tank-pumping truck and covered with fecal matter. And suddenly everyone is in deep doo-doo when a seemingly unrelated event pivots everything unnervingly to hell and gone.

Leading up to that pivoting plot point is some fun dialogue: a motorcyclist has been arrested in Texas for going 206 MPH. The counselor tells the biker's mother, a hard mama played by Rosie Perez, "Two oh six. That's not a speed, that's a time of day. Or somebody's weight. Are you telling me he was going two hundred and six miles an hour? In what?"

She answers, "On that Jap bike of his." Later in the conversation, she offers to fellate him for the $400 fine.

He tells her, as he zips up his briefcase, "You'd still owe me three-eighty." The jailed biker was to deliver a component that would have facilitated the drug deal by allowing the now-ailing truck to run. When the biker is clotheslined by a third party, this is now in question. Someone else now has the component. The counselor is suspected of a double-cross by the cartel.

As Brad Pitt's character, Westray, tells the counselor, "They [the cartel] don't really believe in coincidences. They've heard of them. They've just never seen one."

And this: described very early on (by Reiner) is an ugly device made for killing, technologically quite up-to-date but medieval in its grotesquery. Also, it foretells a no-return, no-way-out absolutism. And it is awful.

Westray, a middleman, has told the counselor what he's getting into, and sees a couple of cracks in his façade earlier. When the deal goes south, he is resigned. What will happen, will happen. To all of them. And it, like the device described by Reiner, is horrific. McCarthy doesn't introduce such a device without using it. It's the old rule: You bring a gun onstage in the first act, you'd better fire it in the second.

I won't spoil the denouement, except to say that it is pure Cormac McCarthy. Pure. (Involuntary shudder.) But there are moments in this story that are stunning, gut-clenching, and darkly comedic. The Reiner/Malkina love affair replete with trained cheetahs in the veldt-like atmosphere of the Texas/Mexico borderland, where the expensively jewel-collared cheetahs chase game, catch it, and Malkina watches with her unblinking azure eyes through binoculars, atop an Escalade, while Reiner cooks steaks on a portable grille. Hemingwayesque through a dark lens.

And Malkina takes autoeroticism to an entirely new level and meaning in an astonishing scene with Reiner's Ferrari on a golf course. Reiner says, later, to the counselor, "It was just ... hallucinatory. You see a thing like that, it changes you."

Reiner's nightclubs with fine art and actual race cars hanging on the walls and classic motorcycles scattered about will dilate your pupils, as will the gorgeously-shot camerawork throughout this film.

The word "cautionary" popped up during the counselor's visit to the diamond dealer, when the merchant warns of partaking in a stone's endless destiny. Again, in a conversation with Westray, who says, "Good word, cautionary. In Scots law it defines an instrument in which one person stands as surety for another." And this locks another moving part into place as neatly as synchromesh gears in a Lamborghini.

Caution, curves ahead.

I think those who expected a feet-up-on-the-coffee-table, smooth-ride character arc and Hollywood ending while wiping the dust of popcorn from their hands would be shocked and disappointed. Oh, there's an arc all right, meteoric in its flashy path. But few prevail at the end. Even Malkina is somewhat inconvenienced by it all. Seems maybe only one of the cheetahs made out, a female, with a favorite rock upon which to sun and scan for game.

When subjected to The Everyman-Hero Paradigm based on Joseph Campbell's *The Hero with a Thousand Faces*, the counselor falls short in the twelve steps from Everyman to Hero—unless one has an extreme sense of irony. For instance, step eleven, Resurrection. (The hero faces a life-and-death moment, then proves beyond a doubt that he is changed forever as he evades death again.) Oh, yeah. Changed. The counselor is changed.

I took a screenplay course under the legendary Robert McKee when I lived in Los Angeles. In his ten commandments was this: Thou shalt not write on the nose. Put a subtext under every text. It seems McCarthy does this beautifully as second nature. And, for those who cried, "No plot! No plot!" *The Counselor* exemplifies both The Punitive Plot (*The Treasure of the Sierra Madre*) and The Tragic Plot (*Othello, Hamlet, King Lear*).

Why, after *No Country for Old Men*, did anyone with four brain cells expect there to be a redeemed hero (or even anti-hero) in *The Counselor*? Hmm? Spoilers be damned. See it or read it for the beauty, for the language, for the intricacies and arabesques of malevolence. Then breathe a deep sigh of relief that your life is really rather boring.

I did.

TRUCKERS, EARN WHILE YOU LEARN

*Or, how I escaped government work
and became free as the breeze.*

SWELTERING DAY on the Oklahoma-Texas border, bridge job, late 1950s. Hot and humid, maybe 105 degrees, it was the kind of day where you could lose eight pounds, then make it back up that night with a big steak and six beers. It would be 110 by afternoon. They hadn't yet devised a "comfort index" to make us feel worse, but we knew it was hot. We made frequent stops at the galvanized Igloo for cool water and salt tablets. When I looked out at the big lake, Lake Texoma, sweat would sting my eyes and the vaporous view would shimmer. I held my hard hat under the spigot, splashed water into it, and put it on. Blessed relief for a few seconds, then back to sanding well points.

Without getting into a long explanation of what well points are (boring), they're long tubes with a perforated end that suck water out of the ground around cofferdams (deep holes with pilings in them that have to stay somewhat dry for a while). They require sand around them to remain functional. So, another laborer and I were assigned the idiot work of walking from a large pile of sand with a shovelful of said sand, dump it into the well point hole, repeat. Once that hole was full, you'd go to the next one. There were many. I'd rather be at a rock fight.

About an hour into this, what the older guys called government work, I had resigned myself that my day was to be nothing but this, good lord. I searched my memory for the karmic disturbance I'd made to deserve this.

Then one of the foremen yelled, "Who can drive a truck?" My hand shot up. He handed me some keys. It was a right-to-work state, so though I was a laborer, I became a teamster. Booyah.

The only truck I'd ever driven was the pickup variety; this was a much larger truck. It was a big rig with a flatbed and an extension trailer for hauling steel. You had to climb over a fifty-gallon saddle tank to get up in the thing. I was told to drive to a neighboring town and pick up some generators; off I went. I shifted up and up, but it seemed to remain in low gears, and I couldn't get it to go more than about ten miles an hour. I looked around for clues. There was a handle on the gearshift which I fiddled with, but that just played havoc with what I figured must be the airbrakes—lots of whishing noises and a gauge needle fluttered. Then I spied a red pull button on the shifter, and pulled it—the truck leaped ahead, freed of its lower-gear ranges. Another on-the-job discovery.

I was now hauling ass over a country road. It bounced me so badly I hit my head on the roof; luckily, I was still wearing my hard hat. I slowed a bit. Once I got to the highway though, I punched it again, up to about seventy-five.

A sign said Weigh Station Ahead. This meant nothing to me. I blew past them like the Wabash Cannonball making up time to Atlanta. Some in the glass enclosure waved—

somewhat frantically, it seemed. I waved back. On the return trip, I was loaded with seven generators all chained down (another on-the-job educational session—they had these "boomer" chains with ratchet handles and you tightened them to make sure the chains wouldn't crush parts of the generators—I was ignorant but not stupid, big difference).

Once again, I waved at the friendly guys at the Weigh Station as I screamed past them, the rogue trucker who didn't just break the law but shattered it and left it lying on the roadside. I mean: they could see what I had on the bed, right? Why waste time stopping?

Back on the job site, I casually asked the foreman, "Am I supposed to stop at the weigh stations?" His eyes bugged out. "Are you shitting me?" He stopped what he was doing and gave me his full attention.

"Just kidding," I said. I would stop from now on, empty or loaded. But I was now a marked trucker, with the construction company logo emblazoned on the doors. The highway patrol had been alerted.

Sitting up high in the cab, I was privy to what I called *lookee-downs*. I could see into vehicles that passed me and became aware of what people will do on road trips, maybe to pass the time. Or sometimes to tease truckers. Whatever their motives, they persisted in antics that would dilate my eyeballs, whether they were alone, or in twos and threes. Naked women would drive past and wave. Couples would … couple in various ways. Threesomes would use their imagination to keep their boredom level at bay. Things to do besides play license-plate poker.

On a bright cloudless day, hot wind blowing into the cab, I heard the siren and looked in the rearview at a trooper closing the distance. *Me?* I thought. *Nah, he'll pass.* But he didn't, so I pulled over. Earlier, I had delivered a borrowed piece of equipment called a fairlead to another construction site. This fairlead was used on a big dragline excavator and was heavy enough to require a crane to unload it. My part of this was to lean against a tree, smoke a cigarette, look truckish. I loved this job. Whole days would pass without any real physical labor, and I was racking up good money for college tuition. What fun!

The trooper's mirrored sunglasses reflected two of my smiling faces.

"Yes sir?"

He said nothing, surveyed the empty flatbed, walked around back, and reappeared writing in his ticket book.

"You loading or unloading anything on this vehicle today?" This could be a loaded loading question. I decided to evade it altogether.

"No sir."

"If you hadn't lied to me, I might have gone easy. I saw you unload that equipment over on the construction site. And a truck looks a lot like this likes to play games with the weigh stations. Speeding, too. And you're missing a mud flap, right side. I can only get you for that and the cartage, which is illegal with outta state plates. Here ya go." He ripped the ticket from his book, smiled tightly.

I studied the ticket. It looked like hundreds of dollars. Was this on me? I didn't know. I was crestfallen, driving back to the job.

I gave the ticket to the timekeeper, fully expecting to be docked. He just said, "Yeah, we should've gotten plates changed. Tell the foreman to get a welder to fix that mudflap." And that was that. *I will stop at weigh stations. I will not exceed the speed limit. I will drive with courtesy and goodwill to others. I will do what it takes to avoid government work.* My mantra.

An added benefit to driving the truck: when the labor union guy showed up to pressure me to join, I was able to tell him I was no longer a laborer but had joined the exalted ranks of truckers. He sighed and left me alone.

I learned other things as I drove. I ran out of fuel, for instance. On the side of a highway, I wondered what the heck to do; calling AAA wasn't an option. Another trucker saw the flashing lights and pulled up behind me. I told him my plight. He climbed over the back, looked into the other tank, and turned a valve. It was the connection to the other saddle tank.

"Try it now," he said.

It started after a couple of tries. I avoided his eyes as I felt my face redden.

"Thanks," I muttered.

He just smiled, swung back up to his cab. But I was learning. The process is sometimes painful, but lessons learned on the road stay with you. By the end of summer, I wasn't quite as dumb as I had been. College would be a snap. This other thing wasn't as easy as it had first appeared, far from it.

A serious thing happened toward the end of summer, serious as in life-threatening. I was returning from a city with some equipment, and it had rained during the day. Not much, but just enough to make the dusty dirt road back to the site greasy. I approached the big hill carefully, paused at the top, and looked down. A rickety slat bridge with angle-iron side rails crossed a draw that, though dry, was deep. I started down the road in a higher gear than usual so as not to break what little traction the truck had and aimed for the center of the bridge. The truck yawed sickeningly and I let off the accelerator too late; I was headed for the bridge side or worse, on the driver's side. It was going over.

I slid to the other side, yanked the door open, and jumped, landing on the wood slats of the bridge. It all happened so fast, that, as I regained some breath, I was aware of the truck seesawing slightly to my left, the right rear duals in the air. I smelled fuel. The bridge surface was muddy, and I slipped, sliding as I found my footing. The truck bobbed in the air at an odd angle. Some angle iron had pierced the headlight on the left and another piece had punctured the fuel tank. These flimsy pieces of rusty steel were the only restraints holding the truck from plummeting down into the canyon-like draw.

Shaking, I walked back to the jobsite and into the time-keeper's shack. I was aware of the fans buzzing in there, riffling papers. I told him I had come for the two checks you get on the last day and told him why.

"I wrecked the truck," I said. "It's hung up on the bridge."

He said something I'll never forget. "You didn't wreck it because you don't know how to drive it, did you?"

"Yes. I mean no."

"Well, let's go take a look, see what we can do. That short rain fucked up more than that truck. I'd rather have mud than that slippery skim-type stuff.":

I see it now. Clearly. They positioned a big Caterpillar, maybe a D-9, to one side of the bridge, another, smaller one to the job side. Cables were fastened to the rear axle of the truck and the front frame. The Cat's operators pulled backwards, the angle iron creaked and complained, and the truck slammed down on the bridge surface, rocking. The big Cat pulled it backwards off the bridge. I switched the tank over and drove it back to the site. Shaking.

The damaged tank and the headlight were replaced. The truck sustained some creases and dents; they left them. Battle scars. The bridge was repaired, strengthened. And I drove until summer's end when I had to return to school.

I learned more that summer about life, about myself, than at school. Those lessons are harder to define. And I have a definite respect for *real* truckers, over-the-road drivers.

THOUGHTS THAT COME IN UNBIDDEN FROM THE CLOUDS WHILE MOWING PASTURE AND SPOKEN INTO A SMALL RECORDER

I am twelve. My uncle Pete says to my maternal grandmother, "Come on, Hag. Put an egg in your shoe and beat it." He is dropping her off at Country Club Christian Church on Sunday. She says, "Don't tell him any tacky stories." Meaning me and, of course, he will. He calls her Hag or Chief and she ignores it, but you can tell she thinks it's funny. After we leave, he drives The Yellow Peril (his flashy Packard) down to Union Station to buy a Daily Racing Form and place a couple of bets with his bookie. Then he tells me about a fight he was in the night before at The Blue Goose. He is a wonderful storyteller.

The last line of my screenplay is "Forget it, Jake. It's Sawtelle Koreatown." Now, all I have to do is write a period detective film about Los Angeles. And a vintage crime. Corruption at city hall or some department, bureau, like that.

I always thought it would be neat to be Little Richard's friend. And to *be* Keith Richards.

Never enter a conversation with, "But, officer …" It trips something, a special neuron, makes things difficult.

Rachmaninoff (call me Rocky) was a kind of rascal. He'd come to the house to tune the piano, and we'd get him to play *Concerto #2 in C-Minor*. Because I was a minor. And Daddy was a miner. We had us a time. All we had was shine, but it tasted good mixed up with lemonade. He'd play; we'd dance our fool heads off. None of this is true, but I did think it, and it felt real. I pictured it all, even to Rocky testing keys, Daddy dancing. An aside: I never called my father daddy, we all called him Bud. But I think this stuff while mowing pasture. It's repetitive.

The elephant stands on the iron ball. It's unnatural, uncomfortable, all his big feet together squeezing body parts that way. But he's been taught how to do this, and when he's done it he gets hay. No one is bringing the hay. COVID-19 has made the crowds go away, and there's no money to buy hay. The handlers have gone. The elephant feels uneasy. He looks around. He trumpets. Elephants are tragic wherever the hell they are—in the wild, captive, trained; it's not right. Fuck. That poet Robinson Jeffers was right: humans are definitely inferior to animals and nature. *Inhumanism* he called it. Read more Jeffers—he was onto something.

Farm work is superior to gym work; it doesn't rip or chisel you out but the breathing is better and the results, the strengths and muscle group workouts, are too. And you don't have to wear funny clothes. You can because who watches farm work? The very bored and old folks in rockers.

Mowing registers on my Fitbit, but I doubt it's useful exercise, like spreading gravel with a shovel, or cutting and dragging trees to a brush pile.

If I win the Kerouac Residency I will have to take my support animals, Cash & Millie. We three have never been separated since they were puppies small enough to hold one in each palm. If they say no, well, it's a deal-breaker. If they say yes, I'll have to rent a roadworthy car like a Taurus for the whole time, to drive down there and back, drive to the store once a week. I would soak up the K-vibe in this little house. Write my ass off, like I do now anyway. I'll know in a few days. It could happen.

College years. Sunday morning, Duluth, Minnesota. Industrial district near where I lived while working on the High Bridge. Depressing. Picture a Hopper painting of storefronts and brick buildings, no people. I live in a dollar-a-day flop near the railroad yards. All night, those boxcars bump, thump, grind, squeal. I live in a Hopper painting. With cockroaches. I hide my money in a rusty, unused switching box. I find a cardboard sign that says Do Not Hump. I hang it on my door. It works all too well. What a depressing time.

After a year at the Art Institute, I couldn't get a summer construction job, so I worked at the post office. I had to sign up like I'd be there for life. The main building in KC was huge. In the cavern where I worked, there were slits in the walls all around. "That's where they watch us," a worker told me. I volunteered for loading dock work instead. No one watched you much out there. Fresh air. Good manual labor. Time between trucks.

I didn't invent social distancing, but if there was a sport like that, say the NSDA, I would be the Kansas City Chiefs or Kobe Bryant. I wouldn't even attend my own sculpture shows if I didn't have to.

So this COVID thing that's going on, it changes my lifestyle very little. Except all the hand washing, and spraying packages. I wish the millionaire celebrities would quit saying "We're in this together." If we're in it together, send me a check. Or at least a card. A fucking email.

ERNEST THOMPSON SETON, MALCOLM X, AND ME. A SORT OF BOOK REVIEW.

A FEW BOOKS have cut through the bumps and clutter of my gray matter, made changes up there, negotiated the neural mazes and worn paths of their own. Ernest Thompson Seton's *Wild Animals I Have Known* is one of the earliest. It taught me to regard animals as what they are, not Bambi creatures with happy Disney/Pixar endings. Our fellow passengers on this deteriorating mothership, wild animals are the most admirable of creatures—they put their lives on the line every single day. Root, hog, or die. Birds that are wounded beyond flight join the food chain pretty quickly. Old coyotes grown feeble have no assisted living or Medicaid safety net.

I learned crow calls from that book. I could call crows from across a pasture with a "Come look at this!" three rapid caws repeated. Instead of all the crows flying over to take a gander, they'd send one recon bird (if the call was good enough). That crow would scope out the source of the call, determine it was a human, fly back, and communicate that fact to the others. They would either ignore any future calls or fly away.

I cannot find my boyhood crow call so I'll have to order another online and try my hand and lips at it again. I imagine it will be expensive, having bowed to inflation exponentially. I just looked them up and, good god, they have electronic ones! What would be the fun or accomplishment in that? The breath-driven models look about the same as my old one and can be had for ten bucks up. I'll check eBay.

I have two books by Ernest Thompson Seton. One titled *Rolf in the Woods* ... I don't remember anything about that one except its ornate cover and great bookplate art. Both are quite old. Rolf has an inscription, *Cyril & Mick, 1918.* They are my dad and my aunt. In 1918, they'd have been quite young, three or four. That book has a 1911 copyright.

Wild Animals ... has a barely-legible pencil inscription of August 1918 from Jules (a great-uncle of mine) also *to Cyril & Karleen* (my aunt Mickey), then it is over-inscribed to me *from Aunt May, Dec. 25th, 1950.* Its copyright is 1898. I would have been twelve that Christmas of 1950, and at the age where books were probably quite a disappointment as gifts. Why not a Benjamin air rifle? A Hornet model-airplane engine? A rocket-making set? But this Scribner's book, this collection of animal wisdom, with its gold leaf and embossed cover, its beautiful illustration plates (also by Ernest) is the single most reverberative book of my lifetime, echoing and reechoing down through the years.

Oh, other books of my youth—*Giant; The Great Gatsby; Catcher in the Rye*; the Mickey Spillanes and the Raymond Chandlers; the lurid-covered pocketbooks; the good, the great, the bad, the prurient—all had their effects. The Beat books. Burroughs, Ginsberg, Ferlinghetti, Kerouac. The books of the protest era and Vietnam. Too many to mention. But surely cumulative in my love of words connected and placed with one another to form new chains of thoughts, awe at the writers' ways of using them. Later years brought the pleasures of Didion, McGuane, Barry Hannah, Ann Beattie, Annie Proulx, Cormac McCarthy, and many more. Pure word wizardry.

But the tectonic-upheaval years offered me books that I read to try and understand the world and my small place in it. Books like Marshall McLuhan's *The Medium is the Message* and Viktor Frankl's *Man's Search for Meaning*. Napoleon Hill's *Think and Grow Rich*, Maxwell Maltz's *Psycho-Cybernetics*. Mind-expanding books with deep value and application to more than the moment.

The assassination years (how awful to be able to say that) of JFK, Malcolm X, MLK, RFK brought books and more books. I read them then and I read them now. We had murderous men in government bureaus then. Sociopaths who felt they could right the ship of state just by jettisoning cargo, killing the "dangerous ones." Even our own government admitted that, yes, there was "probably a conspiracy" involved in the death of JFK. Cover-up books like the spurious volumes of The Warren Commission really do speak volumes about that. One must read between the holes, the Arlen Specters, and the magic bullets, the suspension of physics and logic, and counter it with the damning evidence of the Zapruder film, the threatening of witnesses, the coloration of testimony. These books are among the worst ever published. The above few words will be the only review I give that set of horrors, as it galled me to look through them. Out of this scarification of the truth came a book I cannot recommend strongly enough: Sylvia Meagher's even-handed *Accessories After the Fact: The Warren Commission, the Authorities & the Report on the JFK Assassination*. She fine-sifted through the twenty-six volumes and completely destroyed any credibility the report claimed to have. Her book today remains one of the best of the JFK case, standing the test of time and mountains of new information. It's no rush to judgment or a rubber stamp to conspiracy theories. It stands alone.

I related to all the assassinated leaders, except for Malcolm X. He had angered me after Kennedy's death with his famous statement that chickens had come home to roost. He'd missed the point, I felt. He'd muddied the waters. I wanted to know more about him. What was his game?

It turned out he had no game. He was quite real. After his own assassination, I read his autobiography, which was really a collaboration between him and Alex Haley. I had read conflicting things about this man, but no one denied his powerfully charismatic presence, his magnetism, and dedication to cause. It's why they killed him in the end; they couldn't stand his heat, his visceral authenticity. As Maya Angelou said after meeting him, "His aura was too bright ... a hot storm eddied around him ... making my skin contract, and my pores slam shut."

I picked up the autobiography with some trepidation; I didn't want to read about myself as some over-privileged White Devil, and it wasn't about that. I wanted to know more about why he'd distanced himself from the Nation of Islam and why anyone would want him out of the way. I knew why they wanted JFK and eventually MLK gone—they were powerful, they were loved, they were now martyred. Both MLK and RFK would meet the same fate in 1968. Che Guevara was martyred for no real reason that I could see. He wasn't quite what he claimed to be, yet he ended up as a T-shirt symbol for self-styled revolutionaries. I recall an overawed farmer spitting Red Man and saying, "Any preacher with more than two suits is a hypocrite." The same could go for a closet full of berets and Rolex watches. We're all poseurs to some extent; Che was just one of the more successful. Maybe he deserves the T-shirt, the logofication. The deification. Probably as much as Father Junipero Serra deserved sainthood and statues, but that's a whole 'nother complicated essay, with sepia-tinted Jesuits in my own family album, eyes glowing like coals.

I keep veering away, prefacing, ambling, and preambling. I want to get this right. How I feel, and how I felt before and after reading his autobiography. I don't want to preach, or absolve, or misrepresent. The first feeling that comes to me now when I think of, or am reminded of, Malcolm X is admiration. I have saved a magazine picture of him from the sixties; it is a side- view headshot. He is wearing a fedora, a short snap-brimmed hat in the style of the times. He looks like an adman or FBI agent. Many of us did back then—dark suits, skinny ties, fedoras—before we cast off that uniform in favor of others.

I have dug through my books to try and find the 1965 Grove version of the autobiography, but like so many other important books, I may have lent it out or otherwise misplaced it. This is unfortunate because that early edition had an epilogue that said a lot. It had my margin notes of the time, my buts and question marks, which subsided after I was about a quarter of the way into it; I was reading rapt, in thrall, side notes be damned. What could I say in the margins or in a notebook about this man?

Black Americans who read this book, back then and more recently, say it changed their lives. It rocked them high up on some African-American Richter scale of kickass. Lemn Sissay says so. Spike Lee says so. This is a club that doesn't admit me, but I don't require admittance. The book changed my life, too, in that it skewed me to a slightly different reading, as a compass needle might be changed by the introduction of a ferrous metal, or a Geiger counter sounds at a more excited pitch. I don't pretend to understand Malcolm X on the level that Black people do, but I cannot be stopped from admiring the man he became at his zenith, or marveling at his resilience and journey from virulent racist to a more tolerant tone. But only tolerant to tolerance, not oppression. And god knows he was oppressed, as was his family.

The book itself was missing some chapters which only recently have come to light in a sad case involving Rosa Parks and her lawyer Gregory Reed. It appears that Reed may have sold many of Parks' artifacts and memorabilia, valuable items that should have been earmarked for African-American history museums. History lost forever. But that's an ongoing story that unfolds daily. Why it's mentioned here is that Reed bought those Haley/Malcolm X chapters from the Haley Estate in 1992 for more than $100,000. In those days, Reed was known as a "prominent attorney" and his client list, which included Motown greats, was impressive. The chapters were considered too explosive for publication, and they were locked away in Reed's safe. When he declared bankruptcy, the chapters were sold at auction to New York Public Library's Schomburg Center for Research in Black Culture.

Fortunately the pages didn't suffer the same fate as many Rosa Parks' ephemera and books and are deemed an extremely important find. They possibly show, more graphically, why Alex Haley changed his co-authorship to "as told to." He didn't agree with Malcolm X on certain points. And the original publisher, Doubleday (who had advanced $30,000 on the project) canceled when Malcolm X was assassinated, citing fear for the safety of its employees. This has reportedly been regarded as one of the most disastrous, perhaps *the* most disastrous, publishing decisions ever made. Grove Press picked it up and, eventually, six million copies of the book sold by 1977. Plays, movies, and other publicity enhancing events and news items returned it to the bestseller lists, and the book sales increased by 300 percent by 1989.

Max Elbaum wrote in *Revolution in the Air: Sixties Radicals Turn to Lenin, Mao and Che* (2002): "*The Autobiography of Malcolm X* was without question the single most widely read and influential book among young people of all racial backgrounds who went to their first demonstration sometime between 1965 and 1968."

I was hardly a Sixties radical, though I was one of those "young people of all racial backgrounds" who read the book. When I finished it, I was changed. Few books have done that to or for me. I regarded Malcolm X as a stalwart, a man from whom to learn tenets of dignity, perseverance, belief in one's worth. A man to emulate in many ways. To me, he's never been a myth, though some say the book made him one. I disagree. The book showed him in conflicting beliefs, very disappointed in the Nation of Islam's leader, and having to forge ahead with the painful knowledge that the mentor in whom he'd invested so much was not at all who he'd seemed or purported to be. And, as far as desegregation and integration, Malcolm X has been described as "lukewarm." If I was Black, I wouldn't care so much about integration as I would rights. Civil rights. Equal rights. *Human* rights. I think that's what he was after.

His words, "The white liberal differs from the white conservative only in one way: the liberal is more deceitful than the conservative," were not designed to endear him to either group, and to be real frank, he didn't give a rat's ass, and neither do I. We put such foolish and pompous store into "speaking truth to power." Well, he was one who *actually* practiced it daily. Minute by minute. He was a rare man. He didn't spit when he talked or yell curse words to egg himself on.

When he was wiretapped, it's ironic that some of the listeners were reported to surmise that Malcolm X wasn't a firebrand nut, but a rather level-headed leader who just didn't brook a lot of bullshit. (My words, to describe what I read about their feelings.)

When I was about seventeen, I worked in a filling station and a nearby carwash with a Black kid my age. One day when he was running late, he missed the streetcar to take him home, and he asked me if I would drive him to another streetcar stop further down where he could still catch it. We were hauling ass in my old Ford, a cop magnet on its own due to loud pipes and lowering blocks, when we were pulled over by a motorcycle cop.

He asked me some questions, checked the interior, and then said, "Well, it just looked funny, you know, a white and a Negra, driving together." And we were free to go after I explained we were looking to catch his streetcar. I didn't know what to say to the kid, but I could feel the heat in my face. If it made me angry, what did *he* feel? Not much, it turned out. He was used to it. He would have to sit in the rear of that streetcar once we'd caught it.

I hope he read *The Autobiography of Malcolm X.*

GEORGE LOIS MADE ME DO IT

IN ADVERTISING, you win lots of awards. You'd better, if you're a creative: a copywriter, an art director, a creative director, or any number of related titles. "You can't eat awards," you'll be told. "Best of Show for that? My kid could do better." (That, almost out of earshot, but not quite.) "I don't have any clients who let me be creative," goes one lamentation, and often true. But an idea is an idea and even a client who embraces the pedestrian sometimes recognizes and welcomes it.

George Lois said, "The more creative you are the more trouble you're in. You have to be courageous!" No shit. If I could do it over again, I'd thrash right and left, sweep account executives out of the way, bite and kick and growl on my way to the Gold Pencil, the Clio, the Communication Arts Gold. And, looking back, I was often edging toward being fired anyway. Though I did get some of those awards.

A lot of un-PC shit went down back then. Mad Men days, you know. Snap brim fedoras. Skinny ties. We all looked like The Blues Brothers or FBI agents. Both George Lois and I punched out an account executive, for different reasons. Mine was because of a joke which I found quite funny afterward, though the AE was no longer amused. He went to my boss and said, "That lunatic punched me in the nose and I have a client meeting and now my nose is all swollen up like a doorknob."

"Is this true?" asked my boss.

"Yeah, but." There's always a "yeah, but" for these things. What had happened is the AE had wanted a layout dry mounted and flapped for a client meeting and I had complied. It was my layout and headline for an important ad. What the AE did, and I found it hilarious after the fact, was take a similar piece of board, though blank, put a flap on it like the one I'd supplied. Then he called me in and said, "This work is shit. How can I show it to my client?"

I was dumbstruck. I just stood there. Then he brought the flapped blank board over to me and broke it over his knee, threw it across the room.

Nose connected with fist. Pure reflex.

I explained all of this to my boss and didn't get fired. That time.

In the words of Billie Joe Shaver, "The devil made me do it the first time. The second time I done it on my own." Today's politically correct outfit would be apeshit crazy foaming at the mouth. Febrile. Speechless. Pardon me while I savor that image. Oh my. We had it good in the Mad Men days. I offer an oft-quoted ad slogan for a wine from then; "Man Oh Man Oh Manischewitz!" Just those words made a wine famous and cleared the shelves of bottles of an obscure but tasty Concord grape wine. Then, for a decade, it became an honorific for just about anything that used to get a whistle or a shake of the head. It would be said, for instance, when someone made a difficult shot at eightball.

Next door to this agency on Twelfth Street, the one where an account executive sported a new nose look, was a small hotel which housed a pool room, two tough but attractive shoeshine girls, a shoeshine stand, and the girls' "manager." I think he owned the hotel. Some of us would ditch work, shoot eightball, and drink beer in this establishment. The girls ignored us or traded *bon mots* if they were bored, as we were neither big shoeshine tippers nor customers of their more exotic services. Their boss seemed distracted and rarely spoke. Once on my birthday, a friend bought me the two girls' services, but I said, "You don't understand. These two are friends, and I couldn't possibly."

The girls said, "Happy Birthday," and counted their easy money, but did throw in a shoeshine for me and my friend.

We got phone calls over there. One lady or the other would say, "It's for you. You're supposed to be in a meeting," and hand one of us the phone. Their manager remained distracted. Perhaps it was the lack of business. Perhaps we could do a marketing campaign for him. "We shine at what we do," or "Come in for a shine, leave with a smile."

George Lois wrote a book. *Damn Good Advice.* In it he says you can be cautious or you can be creative, but there's no such thing as a cautious creative.

I did an ad for amplifiers that the client so hated, he almost ditched me. I said, "Run this mother; have some cojones. If I had the money, I'd run it for you." He ran it. It got him eight new outlets in Los Angeles and phone calls for more. He said, "I still hate the ad." But he didn't hate the results. Or me. I think he said, "Man Oh Man Oh Manischewitz."

Awards. We all won stuff. Chrome and lucite dust catchers. But some of the awards stand out now as being meaningful. Once, in Wisconsin, I got a presidential (I almost wrote pardon) citation on a literacy campaign. Still proud of that. And when the agency CEO tossed out a print piece of mine in an upcoming show because, "It's black and white. Nothing black and white ever wins." I waited until he'd gone and stuck it back in. It won Best of Show. He never said a word but put the award in a place of honor.

When I had my own shop, I wrote and art directed the work in the beginning to save money. Fewer meetings. Quicker results. And the stuff won more awards, got me more work. Soon, the agency was fourteen people and the headaches grew exponentially. Healthcare. HR problems. Bonus size. Payroll and concomitant growth of salaries. I hired a business guy to run that side of it. He was the wrong guy. This happens when you're not paying attention. I hired another guy to help out with the creative. I wasn't paying attention again. These guys had left failed businesses for a reason. They wanted a paycheck. I realized, finally, I had more of a reason to want to succeed. I was a hard worker as well. Lots of night hours. And sometimes during those hours I'd look around, stretch, and wonder where everyone else was. They had no incentive to bust their ass, and it was too late to figure that in. I was still working when they came to take away the furniture. One client left, and I had re-signed that one days before. I was finishing a last ad for her before I left. That done, I headed for a friend's house for a good night's sleep before I fled to Los Angeles, my tail between my legs.

Do you know how many Denny's there are between KC and LA? A bunch. I felt like family. It was like the movie *Groundhog Day* when I'd park and enter a similar environment time after time, sit at an empty booth, open a book. The same waitress took my order for a Grand Slam, my road food, over and over. Two eggs over hard, two strips of bacon, two sausage links, crispy hash browns, and two fluffy buttermilk pancakes. I was seriously sugared and carbed up by the time I reached Needles, California, so I switched to steak and salad.

It's a long drive from Kansas City to L.A. when all you have for company is your failures and the next Denny's, so I invited George Lois along. If I expected any sympathy from that asshole I was wrong.

"So, George, I'm headed for the land of dreams. What do I do when I get there?"

"What am I, a haruspex?"

"A what?"

"Never mind. Get a job. Freelance. Become a forest ranger. Work in a car wash."

"Gee, thanks. Seriously, man, I could use some help …"

"Wah, wah. Self-pity is the least noble of all human emotions."

"Get the fuck out of my car."

"You mean this Cadillac Limited Eldo Touring Coupe with black matte accents and the smoked windows and the high monthly payments?"

"Kinda cool, though, right?"

"Yeah, for a gynecologist or a guy just got his realtor's license and a full set of Tony Robbins tapes. Or a pimp. You got a fedora with a chrome hatband?"

"Out."

I drove on alone. Passed a promising looking truck stop that said "Prime Rib!" but it wasn't a Denny's. I drove on. Denny's. *Home, home on the road, where the deer and the antelope play, where seldom is heard an ad-guy shitbird and Grand Slams are ready all day.*

I slid into a booth. George slid in beside me. "Grand Slam, eggs over hard," I said. "Nothing for me," George said, after the waitress poured my coffee.

"Hey, it's Mr. Congeniality," I said. "Sit down. Shut up."

"What you do is march in like you own the place. Tell 'em you are there to save their lame asses from mediocrity. That is, if you have any fucking talent."

"I have. I have that. What I don't have is marching bombasticism bordering on mental illness."

"Oooh. Ooh. That sure hurt. How many Clios you got?"

"One."

"I have ... let's see, last count—oh why bother?"

I got to Los Angeles. I spent a couple of days roaming West L.A. and the neighborhood I'd landed in, just off Pico Boulevard. Well-kept yards, lots of stucco, bungalows, sprinkler systems that would whish on and off. I walked a lot. I was here. Now what?

When I was small, on rainy days, my grandmother would give me shoeboxes of old postcards to look through, many of them from Los Angeles. These were hand-tinted postcards, and the colors, I noted now on my walks, were remarkably close to the colors I saw when I lifted up my Ray-Bans and took in the yuccas and various grasses and magic blues of jacaranda. The postcards had settled into my memory system and now I was *in* those *Wish You Were Here* faraway communiqués. The people who had sent them were long dead and so were the people who'd received them. What the hell was I doing here?

After a long conversation with an elderly gent who'd seen my Kansas license plate, I decided on a plan of action. The man had migrated from Kansas during the Dust Bowl, had applied himself, ended up with a couple of motels, sold them, and was living a modestly happy retirement. He'd had less than I coming west. He did it. So could I. I would freelance after a client search. I would also enroll in a Robert McKee screenwriting class—the guy was a legend, the George Lois of screenwriting.

"Nobody's a George Lois of anything but me. I'm the one George Lois."

"Oh—hi, George. Wonder how you'd do out here. Feel the energy?"

"It's probably me. Tell me, is the sky always brown?"

"Back to the Bronx or wherever you hail from ..."

"Bed-Stuy. You'd last about a minute there."

I found some clients. Three or four. Some even paid for the work. It was touch and go. Through other contacts, I met some people. One, Dennis Paine, had an agency in Beverly Hills, and I worked there for a while, mainly on screenplays with him, unpaid but creatively energizing. I liked Dennis a lot—he was from Nocona, Texas and a no-bullshit kind of guy with a great sense of humor. When I told him I was a little worried about recovering financially there, he said, "Look, you drive a nice car, you dress well, you don't have a pot to piss in—you're like all the rest of us out here; you'll do fine" And, eventually, I did.

A lady I'd worked with in Milwaukee set me up with a meeting in Torrance, with a Dick Hackenberg who ran a direct-mail division of Dancer Fitzgerald Sample. He was kind enough to give me a copywriting project. a newsletter for Nokia phones, one of the early entries in cell phones back then. I felt an immediate rapport with him and went away with the desire to do the best I could on the eight-pager for Nokia. I wrote it, designed it, and laid it out graphically. It felt good being back in the saddle on a project for a name like DFS and a sharp guy like

Hackenberg. It had been a copy job, but I took it all the way through art direction as well.

"I wasn't authorized to have this comped up like this, just the copy ..." He was a little startled to see the whole thing in comp form.

"Yeah, I know, but when I got started it didn't take long. I didn't go over the estimate. Is it okay?"

"It's fine. Great. Let me read it more thoroughly."

I wandered around the office, which was a temporary facility in Del Amo Mall while DFS moved into a building across the lot. Dick emerged from his office, which was mostly boxes and manila folders. He said, "Have you got a few minutes? I'd like to run this by the creative director over at the new building."

On the way, he asked, "Now, you designed this, wrote it, did the artwork, the comp? All of it?" I was getting nervous. It seemed as though he doubted it. I explained I'd had an agency of my own and, in the beginning, I'd done the copy and art, sometimes the illustration. Plus, I worked with some good photographers, illustrators, and typesetters who allowed me some leeway in payment if the clients were slow. In advertising, you get a lot of ninety-day pay clients.

"Just wanted to be sure," he said.

We met with the CD, a guy from the Bronx that George Lois would identify with. The short story is: I got hired to write on a major car account. The office was new and staffing. They couldn't even supply me a typewriter. (Pre-computer days. When I did get a computer, the protocol was MS-DOS.) I started with a lined yellow legal pad and some pencils. They paired me with a good Detroit art director named Gale and off we went. In a day or two, we had a TV commercial that made it through the stages and got produced a few weeks later. I got an office with a door I could shut. This was also before the horrible open-office concept where they racked and stacked humans like pipes in a warehouse. I know the reason for "open office." Money. It saves a shitload of money for the big guys to split up. But they are discovering that productivity (money) falls off sharply in rack and stack openness. "But we have meditation chambers, quiet places," they say. Go back to offices, I say. You'll see great work, less sick time. Less churn. Less loss of really good people. Less infection from airborne illnesses. More. Money. Don't take my word for it. Read *Fast Company. Entrepreneur. Forbes.*

Forgive the digression. I've worked both ways. And I *hate* the open office scam. I started in a bull pen in an Omaha ad agency but soon got an office (right, George, I was good; I graduated quickly). Then, a lifetime later, in my pre-retirement days, it started degenerating into low cubicles with little privacy. Thank god I got out before the elbow-to-elbow bullshit.

Anyway, DFS became DFS-Dorland, and that became Saatchi & Saatchi, and we early hires weathered the changes. The only things that changed for us were the brass letters on the outside of the building and more people in the offices. It was a glorious time, as far as I was concerned. Then the strangest thing happened. I got homesick. I had the perfect job, a quiet townhouse in Rancho Palos Verdes, a relatively low-stress life, moderate weather, a Harley for Pacific Coast Highway rides into the sunset, the ocean breeze in my face.

"Kansas? Really?"

"Oh—hi, George. Yeah, Kansas. Coyotes. Horses. I want horses again. Dogs."

"You don't even have brown air over here by the ocean. What's wrong with you?"

"Nothing. Just homesick."

"You gonna stop at every fucking Denny's on the way back?"

"Yes."

"Count me out. I'm gonna write a book. *Damn Good Advice*. I strongly suggest you read it." And he disappeared in a puff of...maybe sulphur.

WHAT IS IT ABOUT MONTANA WRITERS?

LONG BEFORE Amazon, before the open-mouthed bent-neck cell phone stare, the F-word on Oscar night, and other afflictions of these strange days, I worked with a brilliant Montana native named Allen Smith. He'd come to the Milwaukee agency as a tech writer but soon became a creative force of such dimension and color that I was awed and probably a bit hero worshipful. We shared a love of horses, motorcycles, good whiskey, and handsome women. And language.

The advertising agency was a hide-bound industrial agency with accounts like Bucyrus-Erie and Inland Steel, but, somehow, it had acquired Harley-Davidson. Allen and I worked on that account. Willie G. Davidson was a contemporary and supportive of our creative craziness, but the company was still in the firm grip of old-school mentality as was the agency. Allen was nearly fired for producing a radio commercial which referred to the motorcycles as "mothers," and I had bought a trashed police Harley at a precinct auction which, with some outlaw assistance and factory-engine rebuilding, had become a chopper wilder than those in *Easy Rider*, the Fonda/Hopper/Nicholson surprise blockbuster that had appeared on screens that year.

Such liberties with the original design were anathema to the older element at Harley-Davidson and not allowed within the fence at the plant. There were a lot of choppers sitting outside that fence, owned by H-D factory workers.

About that time I discovered Thomas McGuane. His insurgent lifestyle and that of his characters seemed to validate my own unroped behavior. And the way he wrote was, to me, parallel to Allen Smith's inventive and fluid wordplay. Did all Montanans have this magical facility, this word genius?

Harley-Davidson got bought by AMF and went to their agency, I sold my chopper to Milwaukee Outlaws at a bizarre kitchen-table meeting where the treasurer doled out one-hundred-dollar bills, and I loaded up horses, belongings, family, and moved to Kansas City. Allen and I stayed in touch and visited often. He even stopped by McGuane's Raw Deal Ranch on East River Road in Livingston, Montana, (on his way to Pete Story's Ranch, a friend) and took a snapshot of the great writer signing a book to me. Al told him a little about me, and that is reflected in the inscription. I still have that book and photo. *Nobody's Angel.* A title that was apt on several levels.

The next-to-last time I saw Allen was in the Sierra Nevada Mountains where I was holed up writing, on a long vacation from a Los Angeles agency and Allen was shooting scenes with a Mathew Brady-looking collodion-process setup with extended exposure times. He'd become an accomplished art photographer and made large pin-sharp black and white prints. He shot the place; we limited out on trout, cooked some in an iron skillet in bacon grease. I had given up booze by then, but Al had no such addiction, and he nursed a brandy in the twilight, the mountains that hid the Young America Mine, our focal point that evening.

The last time I saw him was in Milwaukee; I'd ridden a New Evolution Engine Harley from KC to his place and wrote this poem as a result of some magical time with him.

Milwaukee, Home of Fog and Harley
(First appeared in Third Wednesday)

I remember globe lights on that low bridge
floating balls of soft white lumens
half a lifetime ago we rode our motorcycles
in the fog, moving slowly, parting mists

not fast, no hurry, the fog a sort of gift
and we came upon a figure in the park a piper
barely seen just a darkness in the gray but
we could make out a silhouetted kilt, the pipes

and we pulled over, shut off the engines and
the lights, heard the sound from that man walking
lost sight of him but not the bleating of the pipes
our ears saw clearly through the vapors and the

undefined was unimportant background only
to the highlands and the softened shrillness
and I had the strong impression that Al and I
and piperman were all the people left on earth.

A tribute to Al, Allen Smith, a transplanted Montanan for whom the right words came so easily that he never wrote a book or much of anything beyond the stirring letters I received from him and copy for motorcycles and earth-movers. His interests lay more in film and photography, and he ran a company named Huckleberry Film for several years in Milwaukee before he passed away. Whenever I was with him, I felt better than not being with him. It's hard to express. I feel somewhat the same when I read pages from Montana authors.

Montana, when you take away the glitz and Hollywood influx, is Kansas with mountains, only colder. Harsh climate, hard work, a bitch. I wonder if Ted Turner spent much time doctoring his fresh-born bison calves in a killer spring ice storm. Pete Story was a cowboy who got wealthy, not a rich guy who got Western. And that whole deal is another essay. But what is it about Montanans and words? They just seem to choose the right ones. Could be the distances. Maybe they get a chance to formulate their thoughts without all the static and noise. One hopes this won't change with the advent of texting and hit-and-run online verbiage.

Montana, 1948, by Larry Watson is a somber, beautifully written novella, and though Watson isn't a Montana native, I include him here as an honorary. Sort of like McGuane who, while born in Michigan, became a fourteen-karat voice of Montana by tenure and devotion to its manifesto. Between them, they wrote a weighty shelf full of stark landscape-burnished wonder, irony, darkness, and humor. Montana style.

Ivan Doig, celebrated expositor of the "lariat proletariat," wrote *Dancing at the Rascal Fair* and *This House of Sky: Landscapes of a Western Mind,* among his stack of classics. His father was a White Sulphur Springs, Montana ranch hand, his mother a ranch cook. He learned reportage and journalism back when reporters had to know the difference between its and it's and could spell. He herded sheep and worked for the Forest Service. As a writer, he won enough awards to fill a sheep camp trailer.

Rick Bass is my friend (on Facebook) and a well-known environmentalist. Montanans have preserved the environment since before they found out it preserves them. He's out there in Yaak after having been Montana State University's first Writer-in-Residence. He wrote *The Book of Yaak, The Lives of Rocks, Why I Came West,* and his most popular book, *Winter Notes from Montana,* among some twenty or so others. When he's not writing or teaching, he's trying to protect his adopted home area from logging and roads.

A few others I know of and admire are James Welch (*Fools Crow, Winter in the Blood*); Hoyt Axton, a Montana songwriter; Charley Pride, who chose Montana after Mississippi (and whose music video I was honored to be involved in, "Just for the Love of It." We shot it right here on Wise Acres in Kansas); and James Lee Burke who lives in Missoula.

If you're in Montana, something quite valuable may be rubbing off on you: a fluency. If you're from there you may have it, a genetic derivation for word ease and storytelling.

Lucky you. On Wikipedia you can find a list of Montana people I hope to read more from: authors, poets, and songwriters alike.

IOWAY PLATES

I HAD A WHITE 1960s Mustang the year Martin Luther King, Jr. was assassinated (didn't just about everybody?) and it had Iowa plates—red letters on white. I built up a "Y" on the plates out of acrylic paints, so they read "IOWAY." Civil disobedience of a mild and passive sort. It was noticed. Once that I know of. A guy on a motorcycle behind me at a stoplight had zeroed in on it, and he was comparing it with other plates in the wait line. He looked quite puzzled. It was a good fake.

For no other reason than that I didn't want to be in Iowa, I'd vowed I'd never live there or Detroit. I did live in Iowa, and later wished I'd attended the Iowa Writers' Workshop. I never lived in Detroit, but I did work there on some Westin Hotels and the Renaissance Center projects. A radio station, too. WOMC. I named it The Big O, and another copywriter came up with the line, "What would Detroit be without the big O? Detrit." A woman nearing child birth named her kid Detrit upon hearing that commercial in the hospital. I digress. I guess he'd be about fifty now. If you're out there, Detrit, I'm not responsible, but I know the guy who is. Oddly enough, he lives in Iowa now after a long stint in Japan. Hell of a creative guy.

The day MLK was shot, my stepfather was in the hospital in KC undergoing a fairly dicey operation, so I made preparations to show up.

I drove my white Mustang with red and white Iowa plates to Kansas City the day after MLK was gunned down in Memphis. The man accused of shooting King, James Earl Ray, also drove a white Mustang, but with white Tennessee plates. Not even the King family believes Ray was the killer but that was the official poop, like Lee Harvey Oswald, like Sirhan Sirhan. Sooner or later, though, this kind of solve 'n' seal propaganda gets a sideways look and a question or two, because none of the "facts" jibe and real facts uncover more real facts. But anyway, I drove from Iowa to KC and when I neared the Country Club Plaza, a famous shopping area there, after skirting burning areas of Downtown and Midtown, I was waved down by a National Guard officer in front of a phalanx of kneeling, aiming marksmen. Aiming at me. I stopped. I was told to get out, hands on my head.

"White Mustang, white plates," he said, after questions, identification, and search. "That's what the whole country is looking for. Sure are a lot of them around."

"Popular vehicle," I said.

"Keep your weapon on the dashboard in plain sight," he said, after examining my sheriff's patrol Get Out of Jail Free card[2] and my Beretta, which I'd had since college days, a loan repayment.

"I can't guarantee that they won't confiscate your piece, but if it's hidden and they find it, they sure as hell will.

---

2 I had such a card due to belonging to the local sheriff's patrol in an auxiliary mounted capacity, being called into service when it became necessary to search for lost persons etc. on horseback in rough country. We also rode in their parades, took part in crowd control practice. See "Racism by Default."

Good luck." He hadn't noticed my Ioway plates other than their similarity to Tennessee plates.

He patted the top of the Mustang, like in a movie, and I drove off. I was stopped once more in Leawood, Kansas, the Kansas City area subdivision where my parents lived. Leawood's police were much more nervous, edgy, and followed me to the door, where I knocked and was admitted by my mother. They then left.

The next day, driving through the Plaza on the way to the hospital, I marveled at how Saigon must have been like this in the beginning,: troop carriers everywhere, weapons bristling, fatigue-dressed foot patrols, police cruising. The sidewalk cafés were fairly full, the mood undampened by the presence. Girls waved at the soldiers. It seemed to me there was an air of forced, nervous gaiety. Parts of the city were burning.

I recalled driving through the same area in a Porsche in earlier days, a car full of Black people pulling up next to me at a light, the driver hollering, "Hey, you one a my boys, right?"

I hollered back, "You bet!" and waved. And the light changed. The guy in my passenger seat, a rabid racist at the time, said. "What the fuck was *that* about?" Many years later, he lived in Los Angeles masquerading, or perhaps transformed, as a stone California liberal who accused *me* of being racist and homophobic, though I am neither and never was. The N-word had come easily to him back in the day. When I'd tried to dissuade him he'd said, "Tell me about it when they're fucking your sister over a garbage can in a back alley."

The incident with the car full of African-Americans in 1960 or so was the result of some beers bought and reciprocated in Milton's Tap Room, a KC jazz hangout, and some good cheer between Black and white patrons. They remembered my car and a friend's red Jaguar XK-140 roadster when we left and joked about it. Not exactly stealth vehicles. That friend got the same treatment when paths crossed. We felt it was progress in the right direction. We enjoyed being accepted as "their boys."

Then Martin Luther King, Jr. was killed. Someone thought he was too powerful, too persuasive, too captivating. Too right on the money. Too dangerous to the bullshit status quo. So he was killed. And I repeat, not by James Earl Ray. Not in my book nor that of many others.

Some intrepid whistleblower may yet give us the answers and end up in prison like Chelsea Manning or Julian Assange, for daring to suggest that war crimes are committed right here. Because, make no mistake, outright war was declared on JFK, MLK, and RFK by some other sets of initials. But to go on about that is tiring, and that's what they rely on, the long attrition, diminished returns on energy expended. Half of those bad boys are dead anyway and in Hell, if there is one. The other half are drooling in hell's waiting room.

The Ioway plates went to Tony Schwartz in New York. Not Tony Schwartz, the ghostwriter of the *Trump: The Art of the Deal* book, but Tony Schwartz, the sound genius who recorded a good deal of New York City and taught at Fordham with his friend Marshall McCluhan.

This Tony wrote books like *Media: the Second God*, an eerily prescient volume, in 1981. I had connected with this great man at a time in my advertising career when I was exploring sound and words, and Schwartz had been responsible for some blockbuster commercials for Coca-Cola and that chilling "Daisy" atomic bomb commercial, the LBJ campaign spot, not to mention hundreds of others.

The photographer Edward Steichen called Tony Schwartz the man "who moved sound recording into the realm of the arts."

Tony was also a talented designer and award-winning poster artist besides being a sound archivist. Or sound activist. The famed artist Ben Shahn told a friend, "Tell Tony, he's my kind of artist, hard boiled and beautiful!" And my kind of mentor.

But Tony, may he rest in peace, deserves an essay all his own. I was so proud to know him, and the Ioway plates were just one of many eclectic and quirky things that passed between us in the mail. When I sent them, I attached a note: *New York, New York, or a village in Ioway, the only difference is the name* ... after the way Sinatra pronounced Iowa in "Lonely Town." We communicated via tapes, phone calls, and postcards. He passed away in 2008. Those license plates may still be somewhere in New York.

R.I.P. Ioway plates and all that they represented to me back then. And now.

LEAVING BILLINGS

It all started with an addiction to skiing. I tried to move to Aspen, this was in the sixties, but no visible means of support existed there. The only job I found was as a farrier's apprentice and that would hardly pay for a house, wife, two kids, some horses, and a barrage of dogs. (That's the noun of assemblage for many dogs. Ours, anyway.) I tried Vermont. The ad agency I contacted in Burlington wrote back, "We love your stuff, but we barely make a living ourselves."

I wrote to agencies all over Colorado, but no deal until I contacted a Denver PR agency whose main Public Relations account was a well-known Colorado beer. That guy said, in essence, we're PR, but we're associated with a small creative shop in Billings, Montana. We like what we've seen of your work, so we'll fly you to Denver if you're interested and we'll talk. Bring more samples.

Since it was only a day trip I packed an attaché case with ads, tapes of commercials, and a couple of reels. And a raffia-wrapped bottle of St. Thomas Bay Rum from Brooks Brothers. I figured I'd splash a little on my face at the airport before they picked me up. Unfortunate last-minute choice. And I forgot to use it at the airport anyway.

The PR man picked me up and we went straight to his office, got some coffee, and he said, "Let's see what you brought."

I clicked open the case and immediately flooded the office with bay-rum aroma to the point of a secretary sticking her head in the open door and saying, "What in the world is that smell?"

The ads and contents of the case were soaked. "But they smell great," the guy said.

"Brooks Brothers," I said. The bottle had exploded on the plane.

He held up one dripping ad with both hands, liked it. The others were stuck together. I handed him some soggy radio commercials, explained what was on them, did the voice and the music, sort of, and then laid a video tape on his desk. He said, "I've seen and smelled enough; let's go to lunch." He told his secretary to open some windows and see what she could do to mitigate the overpowering fragrance, and we left.

Over lunch, he described the Billings, Montana office and how it could be the start of something quite nice with the right leadership. I told him about the horses, two of which I planned to take anywhere I went. He said no problem, he'd make sure they had proper rest and pasture stops along the way, that he'd take care of it. I asked if there was any skiing in Billings. As though it was merely an afterthought or a minor point of interest.

"Sure. Red Lodge is only an hour from Billings. And there are others." In my own mind I'd already accepted. An agency to mold. Skiing. Horses. Montana. Skiing. When I got home, I told my wife about the trip and the offers of R&R for the horses on the way. She was as naïve as I was—I mean we actually thought horses could be a money-making deal, and that's laughably naïve. All we had to do was acquire the right ones, sell them at a huge profit, and buy more for ourselves. Sure they were a lot of work, but wasn't anything that was worthwhile? We'd be breeders, too, and, in Montana, probably cattle ranchers. And skiers. The Big Sky was the limit.

I flew home. (I checked the aromatic attaché through so it would ride in the baggage compartment and not become a bay-rum Glade air freshener for the entire cabin) I ordered a bourbon and soda and watched the fleecy tops of the clouds and recalled a record my folks used to play when I was a kid in Tulsa: *Oh, give me land, lots of land under starry skies above. Don't fence me in.*

We discussed it for about ten minutes at home and put the house up for sale. This was no more precipitous than skiing the expert slope of Ajax Mountain in Aspen, which I'd done a number of times and survived with only minor injuries. We had a good, straight-hauling two-horse trailer and we would take Percy and Señor, our most beloved Quarter Horses, with us to Montana. And the kids would love it. We would see the sights, stay in teepee-shaped motels, gape at big concrete dinosaur roadside attractions. It would be educational and great fun as well.

I gave notice at the Iowa agency where I worked, which was going down the tubes anyway. And turned down a pretty good job offer from a Milwaukee agency with an office in Chicago. A job that made a good deal more sense than this optimism-fueled flier.

Then I flew to Montana to spend a week at the fledgling agency before we pulled chocks and hit the road. Fledgling is kind. It was an office in a building that made everything go black and white. It was Sam Spade's office. Pebbled glass in the door. An oscillating fan. Venetian blinds that cast ominous stripes on dusty surfaces. Wooden filing cabinets, all empty. Everything but a candlestick phone and a bottle of cheap whiskey in the bottom desk drawer. The office personnel was me. I looked out at the streets of Billings from a third-story window, and it looked like the town I'd just left. I couldn't see the mountains.

Since accounts would be mainly print to begin with, I visited the local printer. And an art studio. The only games in town and somewhat unprepossessing. Reality began to knock at my optimism like a battering ram. Well, at least land would be cheap, so much of it available, right? Wrong. I contacted a realtor. She was a pleasant lady but she combined reality with realty pretty quickly, and I found that homes cost the same here as anywhere else—a lot. And land was expensive too. I went back to the office and sat behind the desk, looking at the Spade & Archer pebble glass window in the anteroom door. A shadow appeared on the other side. In a Bogart movie it would be Peter Lorre, Sydney Greenstreet, or Lauren Bacall. It was a deliveryman. He dropped off a pile of media spec and rate books.

I called home.

"Listen, we might want to rethink this job deal, this move. It was kind of Ready, Fire, Aim, you know?"

She said the house had sold, first day on the market.

"Hmm."

After a week in the new office and continental breakfasts at the motel, I flew ... home and spilled the whole "oops" feeling about the job. I called Milwaukee and asked if the offer was still open. It was. I called Denver and told them I'd had second thoughts. They were puzzled but quite nice about it and asked if I could put in it in writing, which I did.

They just wanted to understand. So did I. Many years later I wrote a poem about it. It may have been that leaving Billings was when I began to grow up. Not a lot, but one must start somewhere and the experience made an impression on me. Billings was not where I was supposed to be at that point in my life, perhaps later, but one runs out of years. At any rate, I've been in rural Kansas for the last thirty-four years. I guess that's where I'm supposed to be.

Leaving Billings

I deplaned in Billings and I walked
to the airport, this was in the Sixties,
and I passed through a gate in a tall
chain link fence. A Black man clung
to the fence on the side that kept him
off the tarmac, and he said to me in
a wistful way, "Someday I'll get out
of here." I nodded, said, "Good luck"
and waited for my ride. A few days
later I could have been him. I fled
for reasons of my own before I was
caught clinging to that fence on the
wrong side of traveling, watching
the silver birds take off without me.

I left other places. I left Los Angeles, though I was doing well there at a very large agency. I left Maui, where I was in the process of working at—and trying to buy, with all its debt—an agency. I kept leaving Kansas City, but, in the end, returned. I have outlived a dozen horses here, a lot of beloved dogs, people whom I miss every day. I write. I sculpt. My wife still works and she creates jewelry as well, stunning pieces, as an accomplished and talented silversmith.

I'd never have met her if I'd stayed in Billings. So, leaving was the right thing to do. What wasn't right was wasting good people's time and effort, pursuing something indefinable for the sake of pursuit. It's been a long journey home, and a long journey since I've been here. That'll make sense to some who have journeyed in place. And to Hunter S. Thompson who offered this line, "All my life my heart has sought a thing I cannot name," which he attributed to a remembered line of a long-forgotten poem. I get it, but I don't dwell on it. As for skiing, I'm still up for it, but my knees aren't.

When I first encountered Billings, it was some 50,000 people. It's well over double that now, with a thriving arts community and a young downtown vibe. It's full of music and sleek architecture and Montanans, both born and transplanted. It looks like a great place to live. Like a lot of towns bubbling over with pride in their past, creative energy, microbreweries, artisanal coffee, parking garages, and installation art. All good things if they bring people together and add to goodwill. I think they do. We need more of that, these days.

SKI. IF YOU CAN.
ALL YOU CAN.

BUT TAKE LESSONS and stay in some semblance of what we call shape. You know, not gym-abs shape but not pinch-a-handful shape, not breathe-heavy-on-one-flight-of-stairs shape. Flexibility is good. Balance. Beyond that, it's back to the title; once you *can* ski, ski all you can. It's a sport that takes plenty of doing to improve, but the practice is so damn much fun. You're not out to capture a downhill record in the Winter Olympics. But you are out for exhilaration and to "slip the surly bonds of Earth," or feel like you have. That is, if you become addicted as did I.

I'm looking back, way back, but with a smile. I just turned eighty-one, and my skiing days are behind me. I can't fall a lot. I'm not a stunt man. A fall past a certain age, for some folks, is truly life-changing. And my knees, well I use CBD, Blue Stop Max ointment, Arnica, whatever relieves for a while. Ibuprofen or Aleve sometimes, though I try to stay away from those just on general principle. I walk. A hell of a lot. At least ten thousand steps a day, often twelve or thirteen. My Fitbit stats say I've walked more than four million steps since last birthday, when my wife gave me that wrist device to get me up off my butt and away from the MacBook some. I'm a writer and a sculptor. Writing is like no exercise, and welding steel is some but it doesn't count for much. It's hot and sweaty part of the year, but not in a good-sauna way—more like grinder-dust-in-the-pores way.

So I walk. Blizzard, rain, heat wave. I walk slower in extreme weather, I hydrate, I take breaks, but, like skiing back in the day, if I'm alive, I do it. Oh and by the way, when I hydrate, it's grape juice or iced tea or RC Cola. I can do that. I'm freaking eighty-one and don't go for all that water bullshit. Sometimes Powerade when it's really hot and I need to replace my sports ions or whatever. And I eat a boatload of broccoli (stalks and all) and carrots every night. *Every* night. Along with chicken and pasta. An apple, an orange, and some protein, maybe a link sausage every day about noonish. Cheerios, a banana for breakfast. Blueberries, if they aren't charging a dime a berry. Coffee until jangling. A handful of vitamins which may or may not do jack. All the rest is bullshit. "The Wellness Industry" and Big Ugly Pharma—they're after us. Thank god for the mute button on the TV remote. I had a physical years ago and the doc said he was prescribing some pill or another for my LDL count which was borderline, anyway. I said, "Don't bother, I'm not taking it."

He said, "Right, I don't use meds either." And that was that.

Sometimes, my wife cooks tuna or mahi-mahi or salmon. I pile on my broccoli and carrots and some of her asparagus. She's about five two and one-hundred-five pounds; she used to ski a lot, too. When I first saw her fifty years ago, I was weak in the knees (could be where my knee problem started) as she's part Cherokee (her grandmother was full) and Gorgeous, capital G. Still is.

I know some of my knee problems stem from skiing dumbass on expert slopes when I was no expert. I felt I was indestructible. I rodeoed. Bull riding before the advent of flak jackets and helmets. I rode choppers and partied while I did it, a lethal admixture. As Mickey Mantle said, "If I knew I was going to live this long, I'd have taken better care of myself." There was a point when the smart money would have said *he won't get through his thirties*. But they're gone. I quit smoking thirty-five years ago, when my wife did. She didn't push for me to, I just did it. I wasn't going to go outside in the yard just to smoke, though she even said I could smoke inside if I wanted. She's so cool. I quit drinking maybe forty years ago. I'd say those two were major, since I was a "hard drinker," as we lushes were known back in the day. Alcoholics lived under bridges; we "hard drinkers" were just partying. And getting DUIs.

If you're a lush, quit. Ain't no other way. You won't miss it (after a while) and the positives far outweigh the practice. Far, *far* outweigh. My advice: hey, it's free. And quite possibly worth just what you pay for it.

Back to skiing. That was so liberating. So exhilarating. And addictive. I would say it got to me like a first heroin pop. (No, I don't know that for sure.) Endorphins blossomed and carried me like a tide. I'm short, low center of gravity, (good for bull riders and skiers,) plus I was well into martial arts and in as good a shape as booze, cigarettes, and occasional weed allowed, so I was able to catch on quickly. In Aspen, I stalked the little groups with a ski instructor, listened from a distance to the instructor's advice, and watched his or her ducklings attempt to follow those instructions. Then I would attempt my own versions. What I saved on lessons, I blew on gin and tonics.

I did Aspen Highlands as soon as I could, and that area has banks of moguls that are just magic on a good day and teeth-grindingly frustrating on a not-so-good run. It was in the sixties and I thought *Hell, I'll just move here.* The only job I could find was as a farrier's apprentice and the pay was worse than basic. Back to the flatlands. A year or two later, I was staying at the inn the magistrate of Aspen owned, and Hunter S. Thompson was running for sheriff. The magistrate was Guido Meyer, pretty right-of-center, and Thompson was on the far-freak left. I liked Guido a lot, but I sure did want Hunter to be the next sheriff of Pitkin County. I'd move there if I had to rob a bank. I still have his poster on my "Aspen wall" here in Kansas.

Back then, the skis were a little more challenging being long—you measured your ski length by standing arm up, and the ski tip should touch your wrist. I rented skis for a while, then got my first pair of Head Vectors with quick-release bindings and a top-drawer pair of boots. As time went by I gradually got shorter skis and my skiing improved radically, though I'm thankful for those first long skis. They kept me relatively honest and curtailed hot-dogging and showoffsmanship. You had to learn how to *ski*. All over Aspen and Vail and the coppers and leads and other areas. Back in Nebraska, we used a ski hill in Council Bluffs, Iowa that had been designed and laid out by Stein Ericksen. It had rope tows and was bitterly cold, but it was a fix; we took what we could get. And we skied until the mud and rocks scarred our skis. Once, when it snowed heavily in Omaha, we skied on city streets downhill to a bar on Pacific, then got a tow back behind a Jeep, skijoring. By then, the city had spread cinders. There went another pair of Heads.

We skijored behind horses at our place, swinging out on the rope and passing the horse, who bucked and farted, ears pinned, showing displeasure at the move. Then there were all those little stobs and branches sticking out of the snow. Spills were rather unforgiving at times.

There were several of us addicts, and we watched the weather reports with narrowed eyes. The hill at Crescent, Iowa had made snow for a base; now snow was coming. A work-halting, wheel-spinning, head-for-Mt.-Crescent snow. It wasn't Colorado but it was fast (if short), and it was a dose that would work until we could make the drive west. Ski bummery was only an impulse away. Hard to do with mortgage payments and jobs, but very, very tempting. Had Hunter won his election, I'd have taken it as a sign and done odd jobs for Guido until he fired my ass for too much mountain time. My fantasy had me typing pages for Hunter, mowing his lawn, painting the house at Owl Farm.

I even tried to move to any place that had a mountain or two. Vermont, Montana, Colorado, Canada. An advertising agency in Burlington, VT liked my samples but said they were hardly making a living themselves. Colorado was jam-packed with skier/ad people. Canada replied with some possibilities.

Let me explain. Ajax Mountain (it's Aspen Mountain now) deserted on a snowy day: the chairs empty on the cables but moving, gray, ghost-like, in the gathering storm. You ski over a rise barely visible in the yellow/amber goggles and pull up in a hockey stop. The quiet. The chairs are gone; the trees are white; the silent snow is relentless; you wonder how you'll get down. There is no panic. The moment is, well, if you're Elvis, it's a peanut-butter-and-bacon- and-Fritos sandwich. If you're Erroll Garner, it's "Misty" in perfect chords. It's peace.

You know some of the way by heart, so you let gravity pull you a bit and you traverse. It's tricky, but somehow you ease down, down. The snow lets up as you near the middle, and you realize how much work it's been to get here. But now you can actually ski. Not fast, nothing foolhardy, but carve your way down. You're warm inside the jacket. The gaiters have kept snow off your calves and boots, but your jeans are soaked. It's time to leave, get off the mountain. And you do. Falling only once. Then it's either the Chart House or Hotel Jerome. The Jerome will have Hunter's raucous bunch. The Chart House will have steak smells and Manhattans. It's the latter. There must be a way you can move here for good. You stamp your feet, the warmth and noise envelopes you, welcomes you. You sit near some vaguely-familiar skiers and one says, "Join us." And you do.

JUST FOR THE LOVE OF IT

WHY DO YOU do what *you* do?

Me, I'm a writer and a sculptor. When I was trying to get into advertising a lifetime ago, I was a paving field engineer. I liked that, outdoor work and on my own a lot, but my true love was graphic design and illustration (I thought), and one night at a jazz club I was talking to a popular trio's bass player about wanting to change career direction. He recommended a self-help book or two, and he told me how he'd begun playing bass. He'd gotten on a European USO tour as a bass player, yet he had never played bass. He was a pianist. He learned bass on the trip over and during the tour. His audacity triggered my first foray into visualizing. Practice seeing yourself doing what you want to do. Continue visualizing attaining that *place*, that desire, and, in the process, things just seem to snap into prepared grooves. You get help. Something out there points you in right directions.

I'd work at the drawing board nights, revising and reimagining ads and doing my own versions. I wrote headlines and drew and painted and indicated type on ad layouts until the morning hours. I'd had some art school background and I lost myself in preparing a portfolio. Short version: I took the work to a small agricultural ad agency in town and started two weeks later. At more than I'd been making as a field engineer. On the basis of one drawing the creative director had liked. Luck? Probably. But something more mystical had been set in motion by intense *want*. By *try*. It felt like working a dexterity puzzle correctly.

It helps immeasurably if your aim is at something you'd do without pay if you were independently wealthy. I'm anything but that, but I *will* write and sculpt if I'm alive and able. Just for the love of it. Bank on it.

I've made my point and won't belabor it. But a while back, I was sitting at my MacBook and nothing was happening. It was one of those dog-ass days when summer is officially over, but it was still hot and humid and I was vaguely discontented. Too hot to weld my steel stuff. I did what we writers are continually warned not to do; I fell down the rabbit hole online by cruising YouTube. Music stuff. Classic old Janis Joplin, Procol Harum, Erroll Garner. Then bluegrass and C&W, some Jamey Johnson. Up pops an old video I'd all but forgotten, Charley Pride and "Just For The Love Of It."

A song I know well. I heard it nonstop for two days. A message song: sometimes just for the love of it has to carry you through. Poetry, a screenplay, sanding a custom car, no real gratification in sight. So do it for the best reason. For the love of it. The other stuff will come.

I used to work with a digital stock music producer out in Los Angeles. This guy was, is, a legend in this kind of "needle drop" music in that he pioneered all or most of the innovations the stock music business had to offer. The other day he received a Lifetime Achievement Award for his work, which pretty much transformed the industry, that's also known for its exceptionally high production value and musicality across a long mixing board which included big orchestral numbers to house jamz to anything trending at the moment.

His various companies provided music for everything from soft drink commercials to scoring feature-length films. You've heard it, believe me. His name is Jim Long, and I first met him when a group of us from a KC agency traveled to Dallas to talk to him about his radio stations. He owned some of them with Charley Pride.

This agency was known for its unusual creative ads on radio and TV stations, and we worked with Jim targeting media buyers and overall image strengthening. It worked well. Our leader was a genius and so was Jim[3]—of course it worked.

Then we began to be involved in his side business; stock music. So-called needle-drop music. I saw him take that from a fledgling niche business to where it is now. I had left the KC agency by then and worked with him in a freelance capacity in a relationship that lasted years. He'd start a successful company, sell it, and start another. I worked with some of those companies after his departure and became pretty immersed in the business. I believe the music cultivated my ear, among other advantages. Those outfits used top musicians, engineers, and producers. I strongly urge anyone involved in scoring a film or seeking music for any kind of venture to check out the music of companies like FirstCom, Elias, Gotham Music, Who Did That Music, and (yep) *scores* of others.

---

[3] Sadly, Jim passed away in 2022, after a protracted battle with Parkinson's Disease. Typical of Jim, it was a battle; he even joined a Los Angeles fight club and worked valiantly on all aspects of boxing. It helped, but he lost the final bout.

One of Jim's innovations was something we named Liquid Music. It allowed you to slide various components in and out, mute, say, the drums and brass, and just use the strings, or actually create your own track with some of the well-produced sections. He made it easy to play with components and come up with your own sound. We sent out a metal strongbox of music titled Bulletproof—each box had a slug-sized dent in it. And the music inside was fantastic stuff. He covered holidays, patriotic events, and regional music like Southern rock, East Coast trends, grunge, urban to gut-bucket country to symphony orchestra. And it was all beautifully produced. Great music, splendidly soundscaped. You didn't get any better because these were the same studio musicians and vocal backups and engineers who were on the Top 40 charts.

But back to Charley Pride. He made his indelible mark on country music and, being a hell of an athlete, he could just as well have made it in Major League Baseball. At a time when he was considering moving from Nashville to Branson, he met with Jim Long and his Honest Music label. Jim called me in Kansas, asked if I'd be interested in helping put together a music video for Pride and a song titled "Just for the Love of It." It was to be a very budget production. Cheap. Jim Wheeler, a KC-based filmmaker, agreed to shoot the piece at my place to cut costs. He did utilize a full crew out at the farm but managed to bring the video in on budget. We called in a couple favors, and the weather cooperated, too. Speedy Huggins, a KC jazz musician, made a cameo appearance as the father in the song, walking in a wheat field owned by a neighbor. You'll note he's wearing an aloha shirt and a snap brim straw hat, hardly farm garb, but hey, it was budget and Speedy was Speedy.

My wife and I live in a rural community, a very small town. Our little farm, about forty acres, fronts the town square, a grassy area with a flag. Barn, house, some outbuildings, horses, and dogs. When we filmed, Charley walking one fence line, my two Australian Shepherds would always try to be near him when he sang; they loved to hear him sing. That little portion made it onto *Good Morning America*. Made me a little sad to see it today, as those two fine dogs (Jack and Mickey) passed away, and two more (Rocket and Lucy) came and went. Now, Millie and Cash are taking up the doggie baton at Wise Acres. They'd love Charley, too.

Somehow, the cornfield hotline informed a lot of folks what was going on at the place. They began to come like the people in *Close Encounters of the Third Kind* gathered at the Devil's Tower to see the UFO spaceship landing. Between takes, they didn't ask, "Is this Heaven?" as in *Field of Dreams,* but they did ask for snapshots and autographs. What a day. Charley dug it immensely. One very old man limped up out of the canebrake when Charley was singing on a bridge, caused a retake, and told me: "I heard he was here. Do you think he'd give me an autograph?" He did, of course. Walked with the man down the dirt road, and they talked a long time, putting the schedule in danger. Charley loved old folks and little kids best of all.

And I offer the song to anyone trying to get somewhere because sometimes it seems like the only reason you do what you do *is* just for the love of it. And that's good—it'll go a long way toward getting you where you want to go. It got me into one of the biggest ad agencies in the world and a good living for years in Los Angeles.

But keep after it. I got three rejections today, but I also got an acceptance. Rare, when lit reviews often only accept one to three percent of the thousands of manuscripts they receive. But if that acceptance had been the fourth rejection, what would I do, quit? Heck no. I weld. I write. It's what I do. And I'm as old as the guy who appeared in the shot of Charley on the bridge.

Meantime, I write just for the love of it. To see the video, search Charley Pride "Just for the Love of It" on YouTube—remember it's a looonngg time ago, and *way* budget, but just give it a listen. My hope is that it'll inspire you some and you'll like the message. I still do.

I ALWAYS WANTED A JUNKYARD

1955. THE SMELL of a Missouri junkyard in mid-summer: oil, rust, naphtha, rotting upholstery, gasoline, leather, paint, antifreeze, mildew, rubber, solvents, some fetid, expired small animal. Turkey buzzards circle overhead in the smoke-white sky. They are drawn by the sad perfume, the carrion of the lost and the damned.

But there be treasure here.

My young ilk and I aren't welcome. Our uniform and reputation precede us. T-shirt, Levis, ducktail haircut, miserly amounts of money in our pockets. Sometimes we make a substantial purchase, a V8 small block, a transmission, but these are rare. What we want are bargain bumpers in perfect shape, chrome nut covers, hub caps, second carburetors for two-barrel manifolds, replacements for cracked heads.

"Bring yer own fuckin' tools next time," growls the bearded, shirtless, overalled owner. He slams a set of open-end wrenches onto the fender of a flathead Ford and begins to retrieve a throttle linkage. He does this in lieu of lending me the wrenches, but he wants the sale. He squirts penetrating oil on the small bolt heads holding the linkage. The wrench slips once and he says words that foul the still air around us, adding to his sweat and grime-stained overalls. He has fur on his shoulders and back. Grizzly is his spirit animal, though we didn't bother our heads with such notions back then. The linkage flops to the ground beneath the Ford.

"There ya go. Two bucks."

I get on my hands and knees, stretch to reach the linkage behind the front left tire. Two bucks. I could get a new one for four. Two bucks is eight gallons of gas and change. Tips shared by the waitresses at a restaurant where I sometimes bus dishes. Two six-packs. A carton of Luckies. And who knows if the linkage will even work on my Edelbrock intake manifold. Rick, my hot-rod friend, says it will. Still, it's unsatisfactory, this junkyard day. Usually, if left alone, I'd stroll the aisles of cars, check the engines, wheels, body panels, smaller parts like distributors, a radio, good trunk hinges. I'd have found a quarter glinting in the sun. I'd have pulled this linkage myself and paid a buck for it. I'd have peered inside an old LaSalle and seen a first edition advanced readers copy of *The Great Gatsby* inscribed on the frontispiece by Fitzgerald to Hemingway, "Follow this, fish man!" I would toss the book on the counter along with a gearshift knob, a Weber downdraft carburetor, and some head bolts.

"How much?" I'd ask as coolly as possible, but with a post-adolescent break in my voice.

The bearded guy would look annoyed, say, "That carb's almost new. Three bucks." I'd peel three sodden bills from my small roll and lay them on the counter.

Then, I'd wake up just before the *Antiques Roadshow* guy would answer his own rhetorical question, "Would you like to know what that book is worth now, in 2019?"

I have my own junkyard now. We live on a farm and I'm a sculptor of welded steel; I work a lot with old auto parts and body components. My work was described by a Dallas art publication as a cross between Rube Goldberg and John Chamberlain. I like that. A lot.

The junkyard is just west of my wife's studio (she's a silversmith and jewelry designer) and, wisely, when I had the studio built for her, I specified no windows on the west side. There's little attraction in a junkyard, other than to the end user or one of those giant cone-shaped magnets on a cable as it slams into a gaggle of rusty crap. That's attraction; lusty, noisy, immediate. I suppose it'll happen someday to my junkyard. The new owner of the farm and studio will say, "I want every last scrap of this stuff out of here."

Two junkyard gods guard the rusting piles for now. One is a six-foot-tall rusty steel sculpture I bought in Santa Fe off a trailer during Indian Market. The other stands near it and is a rather baleful stone piece from a gallery there. Some junkyards have dogs. Mine has gods. Our Australian Shepherds root around in there from time to time, after rabbits, but they are happy, friendly dogs with no resemblance to those of the junkyard persuasion.

Among the corrugated steel, old lawnmowers, gears, and hot-water tanks of my junkyard is the beacon of inspiration that'll catch a glint of sun and lead me to my next shape. I leave you with a poem I wrote in honor of such salvage.

Rust in Peace

The sculptor has a junkyard
heaps of rust, beautiful colors
fenders, hoods, a water heater
miles of pipe and old tin signs

chrome blazes in the sun and
kids' wagons lay in a pile no one
to scoot or push or pull them
they once were shiny red and

sat under Christmas trees, a bit
of tinsel, some sparkles from the
branches that fell upon the new
surface, wagon awaiting pilot

The sculptor wants a metaphor
and it is all around him flashing
in the sun, rusting in his sleep, he
knows it's here, somewhere in the

unruliness of tangled things and
just what he wanted for his next
piece, a ladder of metal chairs
reaching skyward, but what does

it say? Chairway to Heaven? Is
it really that banal and even so
derivative to take Led Zeppelin's
title and corrupt it for a pun?

Seems like a lot of work for a
play on words so he moves on to
pass stacked square tubing and
heavy tools of very little charm.

Old mining cars, much too heavy
he decides, I'm tired today, maybe
I'll give the welder a rest and the
grinder too. And rust in my sleep.

THE SECOND HAPPIEST DAY: A RECOMMENDATION

I FIRST HEARD the expression from a sometimes sailor who'd had a few boats in his lifetime. "The second happiest day of your life is when you buy your dream boat," he'd said, waiting for me to ask, "Okay, what's the first happiest day of your life?" which I dutifully did. "When you sell the sonofabitch," he'd answered, with more than a tinge of passion. "Believe it," he'd added. Then he applied the axiom to marriage and divorce with even more vehemence. I changed the subject, and we ordered another beer.

I had a second-happiest-day experience myself, very bittersweet, when it was revealed to me that my mother had willed me a car I'd coveted and had tried to buy from the family: a 1966 Cord replica that they'd bought on a whim and had rarely driven.

This car was a supercharged Corvair Spyder powered with memory plastic (dents could supposedly be fixed with a heat gun), a replica made by Glenn Pray in a rehabbed pickle plant in Oklahoma. There were only ninety-seven hand-built models made. It wasn't perfect. It caught fire under the meticulously machined, Art Deco dashboard on a trip to Iowa, but I was able to douse it before too much damage was done. The replacement bearings for a part of the front-wheel drive axle assembly were only available at a small shop in Kansas or special order from *Citroën* in Rennes. If one turned the wheel too sharply, frame members scored the tires from the inside. And so on. Showroom-new it was dangerous and a money pit, albeit a beautiful one that the original designer of the 1930s' Cord, Gordon Beuhrig, sanctioned as commendably copied and detailed. And when it ran right, it ran like a striped-ass ape. A very handsome striped-ass ape.

To shorten a long and episodic tale of discord (yeah, it's a pointedly intended pun): it was a happy day indeed when my dreamboat Cord sold. And it sold for inflation dollars well above its purchase price in the 1960s. More reason to celebrate.

Which is all throat-clearing preamble to the following which is about a book titled *The Second Happiest Day* by one John Phillips. And there's a further preamble to *that*. You're in this far; bear with me.

During World War II, my dad was off on some ship as a radioman. My stepfather worked on the Manhattan Project. My war news came in the form of comics. We kids knew that Hitler and Hirohito and Mussolini were out to kill us, and it wouldn't be far-fetched to say the country was suffering from PTSD after a depression and Pearl Harbor. Comics and books became my safe haven. After The Bomb ended the war, my dad was home, and my stepfather and mother moved us to Tulsa. Older now, I visited my dad, grandmother, and aunt during summers and long holidays. I read my dad's *Esquires* and *True Magazine*s and books that were lying around. The author J.P. Marquand was a favorite of my dad's, and I read all the books. I have an olfactory and auditory sense of the books, too, in that my father's room smelled of pipe tobacco and aftershave, plus there was the jittery clicking of the telegraph key where he taught me (some) Morse Code. I would practice on the key until bored. S.O.S. was what I'd learned, but nobody came. So I'd open an *Argosy Magazine* or a book and read in the overstuffed chair, a buzzing oscillating fan sweeping the room with a cooling breeze.

Forward in time. Above a desk where I write hangs a framed page of typewritten material in all caps as though to emphasize its importance, and it looks as though each letter has been gone over with a fine-point pen. Kind of crazy-looking. It's headed **"JOHN P. MARQUAND"** (not centered, but not flush either) and has the odd legend: **"MR. MARQUAND IS THE SINCLAIR LEWIS OF A SLIGHTLY YOUNGER GENERATION, WHICH DOES NOT MEAN THAT HE RESEMBLES SINCLAIR LEWIS EXCEPT IN THE KIND OF SERVICES HE RENDERS IN AMERICAN LITERATURE. BOTH MEN, AND EACH IN HIS OWN WAY, SEEM TO BE INIMITABLE IN CATCHING THE SIGNIFICANT SPEECH AND MANNERISMS OF THE AMERICAN SOCIETIES THEY CHOOSE TO WRITE ABOUT."**

Then, the line, **FROM: "SO LITTLE TIME" BY JOHN P. MARQUAND.** A paragraph follows.

"HOW DO YOU MEAN," SHE ASKED, "THAT WE DON'T BELONG HERE?"

"IT'S JUST A FEELING," JEFFREY SAID, "IT CAME OVER ME OUT THERE ON THE LAWN, WHEN I SAW ALL OF US—IT WAS A LITTLE ..." HE WALKED OVER TO THE MIRROR. "MAYBE IT'S THESE PICTURES OF TOMBSTONES. IT WAS A LITTLE AS THOUGH WE ALL WERE DEAD , AND DIDN'T KNOW IT."

"JEFF," SHE SAID, "PLEASE ..." THEN HE SAW THAT SHE WAS SMILING AT HIM. "I KNOW WHAT YOU MEAN," SHE SAID, "BUT DON'T BE SO GLOOMY. JUST DON'T SAY WE'RE DEAD."

Then, to the lower right, is J.P. Marquand's signature.

I believe I found this document in the early days of eBay. If I paid ten bucks it was too much, and I'm pretty sure I paid more. And I had it framed. An *Antiques Roadshow* appraiser would say, "Nice frame. The document is worked over with a pen and worthless, though it does look like Marquand's signature."

I just like having a little piece of Marquandia from another era. Someone thought enough of him to go over each capital letter of this thing laboriously with a fine-nib pen and make it look even more squirrelly than it would have otherwise. Then, perhaps, presented it to Marquand at a reading or signing. Or, worse, a cocktail party. Whereupon Marquand dashed off his name at the bottom and possibly thought, *Good Lord, s/he even ended a sentence with a preposition and I'm signing it*. Perhaps he thought of grading it with a large C- at the top.

The year I was born, Marquand won a Pulitzer for *The Late George Apley*, and before that had been successful with his *Mr. Moto* mystery books, most of which became feature films. He wrote for the same magazines as F. Scott Fitzgerald but seemed to escape the high tragedy of the latter's life and demise. Although, he did have bitter stories to tell about his first marriage and his wife's family who felt he was beneath them, writing for money and all.

I read his *Women and Thomas Harrow* while he was still alive in the late fifties and, by then, was firmly in his thrall. I looked forward to his next book. There was to be no next book. Mr. Marquand died in 1960, and I felt the loss.

Sometime after that, I picked up a book at a second-hand store; the title intrigued me. It was, of course, *The Second Happiest Day* by an author I didn't know, John Phillips. It lay neglected for a time, along with its used brothers and sisters, in a stack of to-be-read books. I had thumbed through it at the used bookstore, and something in its pages had rung a small bell. The day I got to it, I picked it up at about noon to read with a sandwich. Time whirled away, and it was dusk when I laid the book down again. I had a faint olfactory hallucination: aftershave and pipe tobacco. I was reminded of that old telegraph key of my father's. I didn't tumble to the name John Phillips being a pen name for weeks, but the words and the elegant way they fit together in this marvelous book could have been Marquand himself. Almost. I felt I had discovered my next favorite author.

He was J.P. Marquand's son and had been known as J.P. Marquand Jr. until he wrote his first novel and took the pen name John Phillips. I don't know if he would have taken it as a compliment that I found his writing so similar to his father's. At any rate, he seemed embarked on a literary career, having been an editor at *Cosmopolitan* until shortly before his first (and only) novel was published by Harper in 1953. He was an advisor to *Paris Review* and also a contributor. But he was to author few, if any, books after *The Second Happiest Day*. I equivocate here because there may be a nonfiction book titled *Dear Parrot*, written in 1973 about the care and feeding of these birds. It is attributed to him in an obituary, and I can find no other mention of his writing.

I am grateful to the Marquands, father *and* son, for raising the bar and sharpening my reading tastes, and in appreciation for the well-written sentence and phrase as a teen and after into my early twenties; they led me to the Updikes, Mailers, and Capotes that my contemporaries were reading. But I wonder if I should return to any of those Marquand books that so captivated me then for a re-read. I re-read McGuane and Didion all the time and find them extremely satisfying. But if I go back further, would there be a danger of a less-than second happiest day? I don't know. But I will recommend them from memory to anyone who would like a literary visit to an elitist class society (often treated satirically by both the Marquands) before, during, and after World War II.

I find it disheartening that all of their books are out of print and the authors largely forgotten. You can still find copies[4], and I suggest you go to the trouble. Your second happiest day for a while, in the literary sense, might be discovering John Phillips. And your happiest (for a while)? Discovering J.P. Marquand, his own grand self.

---

4 I did find a 1953 paperback copy of *The Second Happiest Day* in very good condition for about five dollars, [a Bantam Giant, original price thirty-five cents] and I'm glad I did. I'm enjoying it thoroughly after sixty years. I'm neither in decrepitude nor being overly nostalgic when I say this is a good book. I recommend it highly.

ROCKY AND THE REBEL PUNK

THERE WERE several people in the suburban Kansas City living room. My maternal grandfather and grandmother. My mother, a martini in one hand, cigarette in the other. My stepfather, mixing a drink at the wet bar. My sister. The usual drop-in Sunday drinker or two.

My grandfather snapped the *Kansas City Star* he was reading and made the pronouncement. No one disagreed. The declaration, practically a Papal Bull coming from a man who had once been the Kansas City District Attorney (appointed by Harding, but that's another story) was this: "I'd say this boy is well on his way to being a criminal." "This boy" was me at sixteen. My grandmother pursed her lips and frowned into an old-fashioned.

I had been picked up at a juvenile detention center in downtown Kansas City and delivered to the house by my uncle Pete. Reno Pete. Pete was no stranger to police blotters himself, and that may be why he had been designated to spring me. My crime? I was in a carload of contemporaries that had stopped along the way to add to a growing cache of hubcaps, a form of currency back in the fifties. A couple of the guys had hopped out, jimmied four hubcaps from a new Oldsmobile with large blade screwdrivers, and hopped back in with the precision of an Indy pit crew. We were also drinking beer. When the siren sounded, the driver weighed running for it against the possibility that he may have been speeding and the trunk full of chrome wouldn't be discovered. He pulled over.

A flashlight search produced hubcaps under the front seats, some underfoot on the back floor clanking against empty beer cans. The trunk was a mother lode. I can still hear the driver's voice in my head. "Hubcaps? Officer, I *have* hubcaps. Why would I need more?" We were all charged with theft and underage drinking, deposited at the Downtown Kansas City Police Station, and then transferred to a juvenile center. Cops were not hamstrung by any PC mores back then. I spied a phone while sitting and waiting, got up to make my one call that I'd seen on *Dragnet*, a TV series. A detective said, "What the fuck?" and smacked me with an open hand upside the head, as they say. The message was clear. No phone call. "Sit the fuck down," he requested.

When phone calls *were* allowed, the other guys' parents got them out that night. I was left in for that night and the next. My stepfather was a law-and-order type who occasionally quoted John Wayne.

I recall trying to sleep on a sprung cot the first night, in a communal-barracks-type room. Suddenly a shadowy form loomed over me. I thought *Oh God, here it comes. I will fight to the death.* The form lifted my thin mattress at the foot of the cot, retrieved a pack of cigarettes hidden there, and retreated into the darkness. I don't think I slept that night. The next morning dawned gray, and we were herded to a dining area with those long tables they have in church basements. I sat between two large delinquents who jostled me then took things from my tray. "You want that toast?"

Toast gone like hubcaps in the night. I wasn't hungry anyway. You eat fast in these places or you don't eat.

My name was called midway through the next day, and I was led through barred doors to a waiting area. The jailer looked at a clipboard and chuckled. "Says here that your old man said 'Throw away the key.'" He handed me an envelope with my billfold and a few items in it. I'd changed into what I'd worn the night we were apprehended. Uncle Pete was smoking and talking to a cop he apparently knew. As he walked toward me, he said, over his shoulder, to the cop, "Optimist in the third." Then he turned to me. "Well if it ain't Vito Genovese. You kill anyone in there, jailbird?" Then he mugged a boxing move at me.

We walked away from the grimy halls of detention in the sunshine to The Yellow Peril, as Pete called his flashy Packard convertible. On the drive home, he stopped at Union Station for a Racing Form. He pointed at a phone booth, said, "Bet you didn't know your granddad was at the Union Station Massacre. He was making a phone call, missed the action when the lead started flying—he dropped to the floor of the phone booth. Stayed there." He chuckled. "Smart man, the D.A."

Well the D.A. hadn't liked me since I'd told him he looked just like Harry Truman, which he did. I thought it was a compliment. I knew they were friends. Truman used to sit at the piano at the old house in Independence with my mom as a toddler on his lap and play "The Missouri Waltz." Pete told me that and my grandmother verified it. She was great friends with Bess Truman.

Anyway, I survived the homecoming, and as far as I can remember there were no charges and the incident went away. My stepfather was convinced I was scared straight by my extra time in the slammer, whereas the other guys would recidivate having been let out within hours.

"Guess you learned a lesson. Right, Butch?" I nodded.

"Sure did, sir." He poured another bourbon and lit a cigarette with a practiced move of his Zippo.

But what really made an impression on me was a wild night that the tough-love parents would never even know about. I look back on Rocky and the rebel punk, as it came to be known in my mind, and I see the whole unfolding saga as if were a week ago. It was actually sixty-five years ago. I was sixteen, and driving a 1949 Ford, a car my parents disliked immensely. It was lowered, primered flat black, with speed equipment and loud pipes that could be heard blocks away. I believe to this day that they called the cops on me and, for a while, I was made to install legal mufflers on the Butchmobile. But only for a while. The thing was a cop attractant, muffled or not. What was I to do? James Dean had just starred in *Rebel Without a Cause*; I couldn't be seen in a stock automobile. Or unheard.

On the night in question, I had two passengers, friends Mike and Maury, and the three of us cruised the drive-ins and a high school haunt called Teepee Town, which was a supervised teen meeting place near Southwest High School where dances and other activities occurred. Our school mascot was an Indian, hence Teepee Town, which, come to think of it, didn't sound odd or dorky to us back then. It was just a place on Wornall Road where some action might be found, albeit supervised.

We'd pulled up in front, rough idling and pipes rumbling, three of us in the front seat, posturing as only insecure teens do, devoid of expression, unblinking, cool. About that time, a carload of four guys pulled up next to us. They looked like hoods with their leather jackets, but the car was a new Buick, not a rod at all. The front-seat passenger said, "That old piece a shit is gonna shake its parts off."

Obviously they didn't know that a three-fourths cam made the flathead V8 lope a little. Plus, the dual carburetors needed adjustment. But the gauntlet was thrown.

"It'll beat grandma's go-to-church sedan," I said.

"On three," said the passenger. He held his hand up, slammed the roof on each number he yelled. On three, I laid rubber all the way to the stoplight, which changed to red as we screamed through it. The Buick pulled ahead and edged us over, then we chased them.

My passengers, Mike and Maury, were cheering as we gained on the Buick. Then Mike said, "What if we catch them?" Noting his wisdom, I slowed and slid a right-hand turn. Then I noticed the red light and heard the siren. Maury said, "It's only six blocks to State Line."

State Line Road was, and still is, the actual state line between Missouri and Kansas. The myth that we exploded that night was that if you crossed State Line Road to Kansas, the Missouri cops could not pursue you. We all knew that. It was pretty much gospel in high school. I was headed west; all I had to do was floor it and we were home free in Kansas. Then I would take careful rights and lefts, staying on the Kansas side until we reached The Keyhole, a beer joint that served three-point-two percent beer to anyone over eighteen. It was five percent in Missouri and you had to be twenty-one. We had passed before, so we'd just go to The Keyhole for a congratulatory beer. One problem was my license plate. It was Missouri yellow on black #448888. Well, maybe we were far enough ahead that the cop couldn't see it. I accelerated. So did the cop. State Line was in sight. I ran the stop sign after slowing enough to see it was clear, and then, when across, I began to drive the speed limit. So did the cop. That's when I saw the two Kansas police cars nose to nose, blocking the street.

"They can't do this," said Mike.

"And that guy crossed State Line," said Maury. "You can sue. I think."

I pulled over. Swirling red lights washed the neighborhood. I wouldn't just spend the night in juvey for this. I would probably go to federal prison. Leavenworth was in Kansas.

"You two, sit on the curb," said the Missouri cop. "Now." Mike and Maury complied.

"You. Get out." I complied.

The Kansas cops conferred with the Missouri cop, laughed, and then left. One cop was now going to deal with us. One cop, three criminals. Mike got up from the curb to stretch and our lone, young cop snapped at him to sit the fuck down or get cuffed to the street sign. Mike sat. Mike's father was a judge. Maury's grandfather had occupied the same position as my grandfather, District Attorney. All our families were politicians, with a long past history of senators, judges, and mayors of adjacent cities. My first name was the last name of a Democrat judge who'd been elected thirty-seven years in a row and had a street named after him in the West Bottoms. I don't know if any of that had anything to do with what followed or not. We all knew better than to think it would make a difference in situations like this. It was just history.

The cop had a ticket book out. I waited. He said, "I don't think I have enough tickets in this book for all your violations. Ran two lights, a stop sign, speeding, reckless driving, failure to yield, failure to pull over when lit up ... Jesus, punk, what have you got to say for yourself?"

I looked at the ground.

"Well, punk?"

"Just do what you're going to do," I said, defeated, thinking about jail, loss of car, reporting to a parole officer for life, loss of any and all privileges, loss of girlfriend due to loss of car, all compounded by the monetary cost of a stack of tickets. I'd gotten tickets before and just one was expensive. This would be crazy expensive. I'd be working for nothing for months at my part-time job. How would I even *get* to my job? These things raced through my mind and I was barely listening to the cop who was punctuating what he was saying with "punk," liberally. Mike and Maury were sitting on the curb watching us, mouths open.

"... too much damn paperwork here," he was saying. "So, punk, I'm just gonna let you go."

My mouth was open now. Mike and Maury were looking at each other.

"But you're gonna see me a lot in the future. My name is Rocky, punk. I'm gonna stop you for infractions and just for being behind the wheel. Your license plate is a poker hand, easy to remember. Your car, man, you might as well have a sign on it, primered, loud pipes—arrest me! Arrest me! Dumbass punk."

But I was overjoyed. He was letting me go! I was filled with gratitude. A cop was doing me huge favors. Would a hug be inappropriate?

"What?" was all I could say.

"Take your punk friends, punk, and get back in that jalopy and drive the speed limit out of here. Go home, go to bed. I *will* see you later and often. Rocky is the name. We are gonna get to know each other. Punk."

"Thank you. Rocky. *Mister* Rocky. Sir."

He patted the ticket book against his leg and looked at me for an uncomfortable thirty seconds or so. Then he smiled. Shook his head. And he was gone.

True to his word, I was to see him often. Each time, I was addressed as "punk," to my chagrin, because usually I had passengers or was with my girlfriend. Once at a stoplight on 75th Street, I had one arm around my girl and one hand on the wheel.

"Two hands for beginners, punk!" This from Rocky as he pulled up next to me. Both hands on the wheel, I drove sedately away. My girlfriend asked if I knew that cop. Later, she was to discover I did.

We were parked in an alley behind Southwest High School at night. A flashlight tapped against the window. Once we recovered from the shock, I rolled the window down.

"You like high school, punk?" It was Rocky, of course.

"Not that much, sir."

"Law against parking here, punk. I suggest you move it."

"Yes, sir."

"See you, punk." Big grin.

Once on Meyer Boulevard near Brookside, the now-familiar burst of siren sounded behind me. This time, I had a carload of boys and girls. We were on the way to a drive-in for cokes and burgers. It was a Friday. In the rearview mirror I saw Rocky sauntering up, smiling.

"Everybody out," he said. We all stood on the grass near the curb. Cars slowed down to see what was happening. "Hey there, punk. Open the trunk." I did. He looked around. Then he looked under the front seats, in the back, in the glove box, taking his time. The red lights on his car whirled and advertised a major bust of some kind.

"Okay, punk. Get this heap outta here." And Rocky was gone. Forever. Maybe he got transferred. Maybe he quit or moved. I hope he was never injured in the line of duty or otherwise. After a month or so of not seeing him, I wasn't looking in my rearview mirror quite so often. I drove more carefully—the habit stuck. That day, one of the kids said, "He can't do that. That's harassment."

"Yeah, he can," I said. Mike and Maury agreed.

Maybe Reno Pete had given him a good horse tip. Maybe he just hadn't wanted to do the paperwork. I'll never know, but I remember him almost fondly. Almost.

COME TOGETHER.
RIGHT NOW.

SOME SOUTHERN literary reviews (and this is by no means a criticism) seem to want their followers to brag up their Southern roots, but balance that with (if white) a liberal amount of chagrin and guilt. If Black, or some other jacked-around-with minority, they'd like a bootstrap story, or some seething. The South has a duality to deal with. All of us do.

That's fine. The stories swirling around out there in what I call the New Liberation, the alphabet soup of LGBTQetc, the storied "Come Together Right Now" actually coming about, are legion and welcome. The lit mags are helping. An openness is occurring, a howdy, well met that's real, or trying damned hard to be, the putrid pettiness of political contentiousness aside. I'm talking regular people here, the people who pay the salaries of our public ... servants.

I'm eighty-one. Lived some. Seen some things. I do have a Southern heritage of sorts. I lived in the least populated of all Louisiana parishes as a kid: Tensas Parish, St. Joseph, Louisiana. St. Joe, as I learned to love it and call it. Home for a while. As was Winchester, Kentucky, also home and loved as a child. I learned to cherish rural freedom in these places. Wandering unroped. Unleashed. Discovering.

Enchanted. Imagine a kid moving from what is now Harlem to Tensas Parish. I'll just say I was astounded. In a good way. And now, so proud to be a part of it.

Not too long after those (to me) idyllic Southern interludes, we moved to Tulsa in its boomtown era. Did I love it, too? On walks with my dogs, when the sky is blue and a piston aircraft is buzzing silver, I say to my walking companions, "It's a Tulsa kind of day." I can bestow no finer compliment on a Kansas gravel road walk.

But there was a dark side there. On the whole, great people, white, Black, Indigenous. But now and then, an ugly remark about one of the latter two from an uneducated kid would foul the air. And I found it bizarre that anyone was assigned a different area of the bus than I. I never got that.

My stepfather worked in the oil industry as an electrical engineer, something to do with valves. During the war, he had worked on the Manhattan Project and I saw little of him or my mother in those years. I lived with his parents during that time. My biological father was a radioman on a ship, and I saw virtually none of him until war's end.

I remember when I did, though. It was in the South. I vividly remember the sun coming through the tree canopy over the road in beams, shafts full of haze and stuff that would probably make you sneeze—and in one of these beams standing with a seabag on one shoulder, wearing a sailor suit and the rakish Dixie Cup hat, was my father. I ran and ran until stopped by his body. I'll never forget that. The scary war was over. My dad had found me on the way back to Kansas City, his home. My home once and later. I look back on that scene now and realize the jog in his trip from wherever he'd landed in the U.S. San Diego? To somewhere very South. I smelled shaving lotion and the mustiness of train and bus travel and pipe tobacco. I saw sun. The sun the way Southerners see it. I was proud that we were in it.

Where you live as a child is always a part of you. I'm a writer and a sculptor. I had a sculpture show last year at the KC gallery I've been with for a long time. It was titled, "A Love Letter to Tensas Parish." I was honored to have one of the pieces featured in *64 Parishes,* a handsome magazine published in New Orleans. In the show, I had photos of some folks from St. Joe along with their bios. The mayor, Elvadus Fields; a poet born on the Mayflower Plantation, Garland Strother; and a young LSU grad, Joel Brannan who was building a premium vodka distillery in his home parish. I'd have had a lady resident who'd started a restaurant there and was rehabbing an old mansion as a home for victims of domestic violence, but I couldn't connect with her in time. The parish is full of cool people.

It was an important show for me. A Southern blues band played: John Paul Drum—look him up. You'll like his music. It's the real thing. There was authentic food from the area. The pieces were inspired by my time there.

Years ago, during my college days, I met a girl in Little Rock at a friend's wedding. I transferred to the University of Arkansas from Westminster due to her. No big romantic story there; she married her high school love, I went on to my life, attending the Kansas City Art Institute for a couple of years, took a job in paving of all things, married.

But while in Fayetteville, I felt, again, oddly at home. It was far enough South that most students had that familiar accent and some emphatic things imprinted on me there. One was taking a creative writing class under a Southern author, Francis Irby Gwaltney. I read his *The Numbers of Our Days* and wrote things one writes at that age. He was gracious. Grades were so-so, but not bad. I shared some time with him in a college-town bar, quiet booth, dark place, can't remember what we discussed over beers, but it sure was pleasant. I do know that I felt very fortunate to have a one-on-one with him. He was a true Southern author and one who embraced the Civil Rights Movement of the time. Nice man, soft-spoken, talented. He inspired me as much by his demeanor as by his writing.

I palled around with a friend from El Dorado, Arkansas who seemed always to have guns nearby. He was involved in a scheme where he and a couple of others would buy surplus machine guns which had the barrels welded inactive, then buy new barrels, replace the old, plugged barrels, and sell the now-operative guns to Castro from coastal Florida. Back then, Castro wasn't looked upon as hardcore Communist, and Che Guevara was a dorm-room topic, not yet a T-shirt. The FBI became actively involved. By that time, I'd left and was back in KC as an art student in the late fifties and Beatdom, Vietnam, and Joan Baez were our beer-fueled topics.

Another Fayetteville friend who owned a bar popular with college kids, The Huddle Club, drove a Stutz Bearcat. We would often blast through campus in this open apparition from the past. I left my own jalopy wrapped around a tree in KC so was afoot my last few months at the U of A. Then in Kansas City, I worked odd jobs (some very odd—like night pickup in a funeral home) to help pay my way through the Kansas City Art Institute. So I could get a paving job. Another story altogether.

My great-grandfather, Judge Jules J. Guinotte (for whom I'm named though it's my first name—think that didn't cause some expressions of concern among my contemporaries in Tensas Parish? It also resulted in my nickname, Butch, for many years) was a Democrat elected for forty years in KC I was told he had a slave, Joe. When the slaves were freed, Joe stayed on, took the last name Guinotte. Joe Guinotte and the Judge were friends. They hunted and fished together, got tipsy and took the Dodge to the Little Blue River and did donuts on the ice. Raced boats. They had a pretty good time, I was told. I was also told that when there was a scarlet fever epidemic, the sheriff came to Guinotte Manor to round up Joe and put him in quarantine. The Guinottes requested he not do that, that they would nurse him to health themselves. They used a shotgun to underscore this intention, knowing Joe would surely die in quarantine. The sheriff left, shaking his head. Joe regained his health and drank good bourbon at Guinotte Manor. He is the progenitor of the Omaha Guinottes. Used to be a lot of Guinottes in Omaha, may still be.

I asked my father about this "owning" business. How could someone "own" another human being? He said the Judge had inherited Joe some way or another and he was never "owned." I was quite small when I questioned this. It astounded me then. Now it occupies a place in my mind where things go labeled *I don't know what to make of it.* So slavery and the back of the bus were, to me, as a kid, crazy. No one could explain it to me. Now I know what the particulars are, the economics, all that, but WTF. I live in Kansas. So did John Brown, the abolitionist. And Quantrill, just over the state line, was a psychotic serial and mass murderer. I know all these things. But I can't make any sense out of any of it.

I don't have to. Not anymore. I like to think I made a difference here and there. But I know I came up short. I wrote a piece titled "Racist by Default," which The Good Men Project published. Doesn't make me look all that good, but it's nonfiction. I'm not running for office, so I pretty much told the truth.

Anyway, what started as a paean to what's happening now in the Come Together deal rambles some, but let's do that. Come together. The South is a fantastic place. With skeletons. We've got 'em in all our closets. I'm kind of proud of some of mine. A great-uncle who lived in Miami carried a .38 and sent his garbage out on a fiery raft to a Viking funeral on weekends. He drove a 1955 Chevy in the nineties. He was somehow involved with JMWAVE back in the day. (I drive a 1949 Ford, chopped, '88 Merc in it—looks just like what I drove in high school. Here I come, watch out.) Another ancestor ran guns to Mexico, fixed el presidente's teeth, and was first dentist and Mayor of Independence, Missouri. My grandfather was the DA here, appointed by Harding. He said I'd be a criminal. I'm not.

Come Together. Right now. I've got queer friends (can't get used to saying that; it used to be a pejorative), one trans (she's doing fine now, did okay before transitioning) Black, Asian, Mexican, name it. I guess since I'm old and white, the majority of my friends are, too. Just the way it is.

I was sitting on my chopper back some time ago, stoplight on Vine, in a Black part of town. Black guy walking across, says. "You don't look tough to me." Snarled it. I laughed, said "You're right about that, I'm not." Then he laughed, sort of friendly, and walked on.

Come together. Right now. It's okay. It'll be good.

COVID DAYS, CHOCOLATE NIGHTS

LIVING ON A FARM, I think about New York and L.A. during these quarantine days. I've lived in both those places. In New York, as a child, I remember the front stoop and how social those stoops were, especially in summer, with the hydrants turned on and kids running through the jets of water; the braver ones ran close to the hydrant catching the brunt of the pressure, while the others made do with the outer sluices of cooling water. This was 120th Street in Manhattan. I would sit, unobserved, listening to older people talk in foreign languages; when they'd laugh I'd laugh, pretending I understood what they'd said. Sometimes this was cause for consternation.

The stoop sitters are probably farther apart now, if outside at all. A NY photographer friend, Wick Beavers, said this in an email today:

From the epicenter:

We may be flat lining on the top of the curve today as the death rate still climbs.

Bet it hits over 800 New Yorkers today.

Sorry about the use of "flat lining."

I'm glad I finally went back to college and learned the difference between acceleration and speed.

Wanted to say if anyone has ever wondered what crossing an ocean on a sailboat is like: if you're sheltering in place, you may be beginning to get the idea.

Without the rolling and the sound of water rushing underneath you as you fight for sleep and dream of still calm dry land. And humans outside your pod.

You hope the stores hang on, the time passes quickly and the boat- and its systems- don't fail you. You've got a pretty extensive spare parts kit but ...

You watch four hours on, four off if you're doing it with your spouse/partner. You eat when you should be sleeping, you check the bilge for water, you check the horizon and you plot yourself on the unimaginably large South Pacific Ocean chart. Every four hours.

At night, you check the radar for transecting squalls and other yachts that might suddenly end your family's future.

And you fight the fatigue until 4 a.m. when your watch is over.

But really? A lot of it is just holding on. The floor, the deck, the boat never stop moving. It's work. You just don't realize how much this affects you psychically.

The streets are very quiet these days so the whoop whoop staccato punctuation of ambulance sirens every five to ten minutes is rattling.

I'm beginning to wonder if Corona can go airborne to the second floor? Shall I shut the windows?

You learn, like the rolling, to live with it.

It's 7 p.m. now and the anxious folk in the city are getting their ya-ya's going. They go to the windows and work their vocal cords.

I've never heard my neighbor's voice.

Wish I had a West Marine fog horn. A cherry bomb! Even the dogs are barking ... Cacophonous mayhem and gleeful delivery is good!

I'm sure Samaritan's Purse Tent City out in the park nearby can hear this.

If they're not on ventilators in induced comas.

Maybe just try to think of this as your seventh day on a trip from the Galapagos to the Marquesas.

We're on passage in the trades.

That's what it felt like to me today in the epicenter.

Hang on.

What's the alternative?

Stay well.

Los Angeles was so different. I was much older and lived in the South Bay. I could see the ocean from my place, a rented townhouse. Everything was at a premium out there. I made good money but couldn't find a way to own a home, nor did I want to when I considered the impermanence I felt there. At my desk (we had offices back then, not the ungodly rack and stack elbow-to-elbow workplaces of today that employers force people into—veal and pigs and chicken farms come to mind), I had a picture of a horse, an orange-leafed autumn tree, and a long desert highway. These three pictures were stuck together under glass in an easel-backed frame, and served to remind me that, once again, I would own horses, that I would again live where seasons changed, and the highway would be west to east, back to Missouri or Kansas. On the trip I would eat steak, prime rib, and Grand Slam breakfasts. I would drive at a leisurely pace, and I would take Route 66 for some of the trip. I would stop and watch sunsets. During this passage back the way I'd come, I would listen to 40s jazz and 50s Modern Jazz and Rock and Roll. I did all of that. I was going home on my terms.

I chose a motel in Kansas, contacted a real estate company, and started looking. Prices had escalated in the few years I'd been gone, so I looked farther from Kansas City, fifty miles south, and found a place. The place I'm at now, thirty-four years later. I got married to my best-ever wife and friend thirty-two years ago. We worked and built on to the little one-hundred-year-old farmhouse and built a studio out back. Some acres right out the front door had been held back because the seller wanted his son to build there; when that didn't happen, he finally sold them to me. And I bought another landlocked sixteen acres adjoining the north pasture. All told, it adds up to about forty acres. A rancher friend hays it in round bales; while the horses were alive, he also furnished a hundred square bales from the brome pasture grass they liked, and we stacked it in the barn. The barn was built in 1894. Fresh brome hay in a dark barn—what a great smell.

This is where we self-isolate. I'm retired, and my wife still works—from home now. I watched our retirement fund go to half and it wasn't great to begin with. I'm a poet, writer, and sculptor. Had a solo show coming up May 1st, but the gallery called and said it would be postponed to June 5th. I don't yet know if that's realistic or optimistic. Or if there will be a gallery. They operate pretty close to the bone.

Today, I mowed. That took a while. Then I cut trash trees and storm-downed trees, dragged them to a brush pile in the pasture. The pasture is greening nicely. It was good to be out. The chainsaw blade came off and that took a half-hour or so to fix and retighten. All this was keeping me from thinking too much. The pups were playing and having a great time, tumbling and running. The last horse passed away a year ago March, a gentle mare who'd been a polo pony, agile and willing. She's buried on the south side of the pond with some of her friends: Harley, Mighty Mouse, Lopez, and Dutch. Some came here as colts, spent their lives at Wise Acres. They enjoyed their time and place. Who could ask for more?

Today Was a Good Day

I dislike honoring the current thing
with poetry but since it's affecting
everyone's daily life I can't help at
least acknowledging the scourge

the root word of pandemic is *all* as
is the root of pandemonium, but the
latter has even more evil attached
because of demonium and hell but

the words might mean the same yet
one is quieter, insidious like a gas
that silently spreads its awful wings
and brings down all including kings

But today, I have to say, was just a
day of satisfaction, cutting nuisance
trees like thorns and piss elms and
dragging to a brush pile out in the

pasture, treating stumps to kill them
off, cleaning out the old corral that
kept my horses in a bunch for vets
and farriers to treat and trim, then

the triumphal release, the open gate
the thunder of vamoose drumming
the air, but now they have escaped
it all, whinnying in a better place

I miss them, but the pups are here
to walk with me and elicit laughter
with their antics, and brisk walks
suit us, raise our heartbeats, raise

my old body's resistance to a vile
and democratic apolitical disease
then I take a long hot bath, count
my blessings. It was a lovely day.

My wife, Freddie, baked some chicken earlier in the week and there's broccoli and carrots. I'm hungry. We'll watch *Masterpiece Theater* on KCPT, which our outside aerial picks up. And, in the freezer, there's some ice cream a local dairy makes called "Chocolate to Die For." I'm unsure of the marketing effectiveness of this name, but it's the only ice cream I've ever seen that's as dark chocolate inside the package as it is on the photo outside. And is it good! Not much left, but enough for tonight.

So, another day toward a future. And a chocolate night. And blessed sleep. May all the people in New York and Los Angeles and in between experience coming days of health and a return of normalcy—and chocolate nights if they want them.

FORGET IT, JAKE. IT'S HOLLYWOOD. A REVIEW.

(A review of Sam Wasson's *The Big Goodbye—Chinatown and the Last Years of Hollywood*)

THE COVER ART of *The Big Goodbye—Chinatown and the Last Years of Hollywood* is a reason I bought this book. It reminded me of Michael Schwab's wonderful art of the seventies, maybe Shepard Fairey, even Banksy—all of whom I am drawn to. (It was designed by Steven Seighman.) Another was the mention of Chinatown, and another was the Chandleresque *Big Goodbye* in the title. It all came together in a gestalt that spoke more than this volume to me. *The Last Years of Hollywood*, not so much. As far as I know, Hollywood is still there and still magnetic, moth-drawing, Schwab Drugstore actress-discovering, myth-making magic.

L.A. waiters and cops and clerks still have screenplays in their back pockets and auditions at 9 a.m., which make them call in sick at their day jobs.

Hollywood, chimeric as it may seem in the cold light of day in Cleveland or Kansas City, is still more substantial than Packard or Studebaker or Kodak or any number of corporeal corporations that were regarded as verities. Whether the film studios are run by bean counters or corporate philistines, the demand for product, *dreams*, is ravenous, good times or bad.

The Wasson book tends to epochize the late sixties/early seventies as an era, a golden age that ended. Eras do end; that's why they call them eras. And a certain period did end, but the subsequent eras were attached like boxcars, and the string of them keeps on rumbling along. Golden Age after Golden Age. Ups and downs. Flops and Blockbusters. The Dream.

Things happen synchronously and legends result. Once upon a time, Jack Nicholson showed up, Robert Towne poured himself into a screenplay, Roman Polanski came along with a large amount of European freight, Edward Taylor, Bob Evans, real estate became available, a studio bigwig was endowed with trust, a woman heard a Bunny Berigan tune from 1937, Faye Dunaway's trajectory coincided, any number of things *happened* that no amount of muscling or straining could have *made* happen, although vast amounts of energy and angst and stress were expended. Jack Nicholson even lost his shit a couple of times, and that man seems to have an endless stress envelope that's hard to breach.

I liked Wasson's book, his writing, for the most part, and his painstaking details from the various lens sizes used in a shot, to descriptions of Woodland, a character in its own right, Evans's chateau in the hills with Mako-designed tennis courts, surrounding pool, and custom poolhouse screening room. The lavish estate was home to more deals than Paramount's offices in its Evans-owned heyday. Originally designed in 1940 by John Woolf, the favorite architect of Fanny Brice and George Cukor, Woodland personified Southern California Regency and each Evans-occupied night there involved a party or a screening of dailies or both.

At party's end, Evans was forced to sell the estate, cocaine always exacting a toll beyond its original cash value. Roman fled to Paris for its non-extradition policy, and Towne struggled with *The Two Jakes*, the second Gittes film in a proposed trilogy. The third was never mentioned again. Nicholson was not unscathed; his grief over the death of John Huston was a long-time healing and the buddy atmosphere of the pre-*Chinatown* group went the way of the third film in the series, *Gittes vs. Gittes*.

Chinatown, its speed bumps and construction, subtexts and metaphors, is the major player in Wasson's *The Big Goodbye*—all the work that went into the film, all the work that was cut out of it, and its collateral damages and collateral gifts. Other subjects are dealt with in various depths: the dealmakers, actors, screenwriters, directors, and producers, as well as Hollywood products like *The Godfather, Shampoo, Jaws,* and *The Conversation. Billy Jack's* strategic ad budget scheme and how it happened would not seem to be of great interest, but as it changed Hollywood's entire advertising and distribution methods it becomes an intriguing sidebar. Insights into the various lives entwined with *Chinatown's* pre-, during, and post-production are both sobering and fascinating.

Wasson did some admirable homework on his subject, and information seekers will be glad to see a full index, "Academy to Zukor," and a fifty-page complement of notes with page numbers.

Edward Taylor remains a benign shadow throughout the writing of *Chinatown* (the screenplay), his contributions or lack of them never fully explained, in part because Taylor himself refused to acknowledge them. His name never appears on the credits, but, again, that could be due to his own wishes. The conclusion a reader is left with is that Taylor was a contributor of some importance if only for moral support, which Towne certainly seemed to need. Even so, the script was lacking coherence and remained unfinished even when shooting began. Polanski was responsible for some of the writing (and rewriting), though we don't know how much or how little. Prior to *Chinatown*, Towne's screenwriting gifts were mainly as a consultant with unusual powers of script revival. We do know that he overwrote *Chinatown* by a hundred or so pages, requiring a drastic slimming regimen. And Nicholson's sharp observations also found their way into the screenplay.

This book with the handsome cover belongs on any cinephile's shelf, as well as in the collections of film students, teachers, filmmakers, and Hollywood cinema history aficionados.

I'd have welcomed it when, after my arrival in Los Angeles, I took a screenwriting story- structure course under Robert McKee—one of the subjects was *Chinatown*. I rented it from Blockbuster Video and must have watched it a dozen times for its various meanings, both hidden and undisguised, and for the Polanski-bleached drought scenes, the dialogue and subtext, and the captivating acting.

Of McKee's Ten Commandments in the syllabus, number IX is "Thou shalt not write on the nose. Put a subtext under every text." *Forget it, Jake. It's Chinatown.* Especially as massaged by Polanski. Quite possibly, the Wasson book would have been in McKee's syllabus on page ten, Recommended Reading List.

I did a lot of walking in West L.A.: San Pedro, Palos Verdes, Manhattan Beach, Venice Beach, Santa Monica, Westwood, Hollywood, Beverly Hills, Torrance, Culver City—glamour spots and those with nothing in particular to recommend them. I saw Polanski's colors in all of them. I saw the colors of hand-tinted postcards from the 1920s and 1930s, and they were the true colors of the movie, *Chinatown*. I saw them through Jack Nicholson's Ray-Bans. I wanted to live in that little complex where Ida Sessions' body was found. I very nearly moved to San Pedro but settled instead on Rancho Palos Verdes since it was closer to a job I had in Torrance. I saw L.A. through a *Chinatown* lens, yet I never saw much of actual Chinatown at all. Take a look at Robert McKee's YouTube precis of *Chinatown* by VHS Video Vault.

I recommend reading Sam Wasson's engaging, even poetic, book, but never believe that it chronicles "The Last Years of Hollywood." That would be to say The Dream is finite. As Wasson himself says, "'In Woodland, there are still roses ...'" And, as a businessman said, in Wasson's book, "'I've been to Paris, France, and I've been to Paramount's Paris. Paramount's is better.'"

MAKE ME AN ANGEL

JOHN PRINE, MAN. What can you say about him that hasn't been said a dozen ways already? Well, that doesn't negate the need or will to say it. So, instead of getting all elegiac on your ass, this is just a ramble. A look back. Back when tapes were a thing, I'd make up tapes to play in my truck, especially when I lived up north in polka-land. John Prine was always on these tapes along with Chris LeDoux (I once heard a C&W DJ say, "Who is this Chris LeDoux? Some listener called in and complained we never play him ..." That was in Kansas City. I avoided that station from then on. He probably would have said that about Billy Joe Shaver or John Prine. If you're in the business you ought to have some background, not just a playlist issued by your Top 40 or C&W station. Background. Love of what you do. Respect for it.)

The last time I saw him was on that terrific public television show, *Austin City Limits*, a rerun, and he looked like he did on his last album cover, *The Tree of Forgiveness*, like he'd been through a lot but he was pure-D John Prine to his very boot soles, and that crowd was there because he was there. He said one of the cancer bouts that he'd survived had made his voice a little deeper, huskier, and he liked it that way. It didn't slow him down much. He was a lot of places. Coachella, New Zealand, Brooklyn, Kentucky, Canada, Denmark, Berlin, U.K., Belgium, France, British Columbia, all over. Then his heart needed some fixing and this god-awful COVID-19 shit that slammed us all to a screeching standstill and killed millions snuck in, and he couldn't make it through the double whammy. He'd have written a pretty good song about it, using all of his most powerful tools: pathos, humor, genius combinations of words that nobody else could ever think up.

I read somewhere that he'd sing and play in a closet when he was growing up so that if he ever went blind he could still go at it. When a lot of kids were reading beneath the covers with a flashlight, I had an old Emerson Bakelite radio in there with me at night, listening to XERF Del Rio, Texas, the clear channel border-blasting gospel and hillbilly music station (I was in Tulsa in the late 1940s, and it came in strong) and KVOO Tulsa, listening to Webb Pierce and Lefty Frizzell. I couldn't carry a tune in a lard can but I could listen, and I was deeply affected by the same music that was seeping into Prine's consciousness, his fingers, his synapses, and one-of-a-kind musicality. Then later in life, I heard him and his songs and said, *Thank You, music gods!*

A typical truck tape (I was able to locate six of these dusty old mixtapes from a stash of about one hundred that have been left from Jackson, Michigan to Monroe, Louisiana) lists John Prine's "Be My Friend Tonight," alongside R.E.M., Kazumi Watanabe, Lyle Lovett, Billy Joe Shaver, Nanci Griffith, Ricky Skaggs, Freddie Mercury, and Depeche Mode. Eclectic.

Another tape has him among The Church, Chuck Berry, Springsteen, Willie, Waylon, Chris, Pat Metheny, and Los Lobos. Any more, when I drive, I just listen to *Sports Talk* and CDs. No one's gonna please me up and down the dial, not even the pay radio SiriusXM that my wife likes on in her Jeep. Unless they had a John Prine station with every fourth song being The Crystal Method or Tony Joe White. Three Prines and a crazy synth item followed by three more Prines and a Cole Porter would be about right.

I had CDs made up special when I was still doing radio commercials or TV sound at the studios—one might be just Prine alternating with David Allan Coe and a Kansas City Jazz outfit named City Lights Orchestra with David Basse singing. I might be attention-deficient like to keep changing it up, but John Prine just knocks me out, song after song after song.

Sorry I have to keep putting this in terms of *me,* but I'm just trying to evoke what effect he's had on me—we know the indelible imprint he's made on folk, rock, Nashville, and other aesthetics. As a poet with some books published, I will claim some familiarity with wordplay and cadence and I hold him and the two Dylans in absolute awe. Another of my very favorite poets is Ted Kooser, a U.S. Poet Laureate. It's quite fitting to me that, in 2005, at Kooser's request, Prine became the first singer-songwriter to read and perform at The Library of Congress. What an honor. Ted Kooser, who will surely take his place next to Robert Frost as one of the greatest poets of all time, recognized greatness in John Prine's work. His poetry. Wow. That, to me, ranks right up there with all of Prine's many Emmy wins and nominations.

I never met him, but I know him, or think I do. I know him from the words, the kindness, and humanness behind many of them, what the other legends say about him, who he mentored, his path. Man, what a life. What gifts he gave and had. He gave me this:

Make me an angel
That flies from Montgomery
Make me a poster
Of an old rodeo ...

Haunting. Unforgettable. I love it whoever does it, but an Atlanta group called Foxes and Fossils performed a tribute version that I kind of dug, being a fossil. Maybe you will too. If not, guess what? You'll find plenty of covers out there, not the least of which is Ms. Raitt's.

And he gave me "Hello in There" which resonates a bit differently with me now than it did fifty years ago. Let that one sink in. My goodness.

My wife is a fan too. She downloaded his latest album before he passed away onto her iPhone and John goes with her when she walks every day. *Tree of Forgiveness*. When I told her what I was writing, she plunked that phone down beside me and dialed him in. I'm listening to "Knockin' on Your Screen Door" right now. It could be a good street busker on a corner in Birmingham or Memphis, but for the giveaway sleek, yet not overly lush, Nashville arrangement. Beautiful.

"God Only Knows" seems simplistic, but, like a lot of Prine, it will probably gain meaning with listening. "God only knows the price that you pay for the ones you hurt along the way" or "God only knows that I'm not true to the things I say and the things I do" carries a stringent sting in these days after the unbelievable death of George Floyd. God knows Prine would have had some deeply-felt words about that.

"When I Get to Heaven" starts with a harp thrum straight out of a Cary Grant movie, then he poeticizes about a vodka and ginger ale and smoking a cigarette that's nine miles long. Seeing all his mama's sisters. And his old man saying, "Buddy, when you're dead, you're a dead peckerhead," and proving him wrong. Only Prine could think of kissing a pretty girl on the Tilt-A-Whirl—what imagery! What energy and color! Man oh man. If there is a heaven, and I sure hope there is, he's there. And the concerts are free.

LYING FOR FUN AND PROFIT

You already know what comes next. I'm a fiction writer. So I make stuff up out of whole cloth. (What does that mean, anyway? Whole cloth is real, so if you make stuff up out of it, why is that not real? I Googled it, but it's not all that interesting: it seems tailors used to be liars too. They'd advertise suits made of "whole cloth" while they were actually made of pieced-together cloth. Big deal.) And I write nonfiction and poetry too. Nonfiction should be pretty close to the truth, and poetry, well, it can be incomprehensible. Mine isn't, by the way—I'm not that smart. But all the great poetry lately is enigmatic (to me) but full of angst. Seething,

Anyway. I told some lies the other day that made me laugh. I was walking and started laughing, and that makes dogs bark, but I found it funny, the lies. Let me explain. If I meet someone new, I always tell them some outrageous lie and ask that they keep it secret, and then if it gets around and comes back to me, I know they spilled it.

This very enthusiastic guy I met told me out-of-school things that required me to answer in kind. So, I said my first wife was an unrepentant cheater and our two or three children (it's been said I'm out of touch with my kids) aren't really mine. That one hasn't come back yet, maybe because it's just not that interesting. One that did, however, is: "Don't tell anyone, but I killed a man in Omaha. Beat him with a barstool. I paid my debt to society, did time. But I got out early for good behavior and for singing for the governor of Nebraska."

"That's incredible. What did you sing?"

"'Another Man Done Gone' and 'Bully of the Town.'"

"Golly. Can you sing them for me?"

"I hardly think so."

"What prison was it?"

"Angola. I don't know. That time back then is not very accessible. You understand."

"Isn't Angola in Louisiana?"

"You're kind of a stickler for details, aren't you?"

"I don't mean to pry ..."

"See this barstool?"

"That one came back to me in a strange way. The bartender at The Flamingo said, 'You know the barstools here are anchored to the floor.' Another beer?"

I told a whole lot of lies in a thriller novel about New Orleans and the Marais des Cygnes National Wildlife Refuge in Kansas. It was fun, but not much profit. I made stuff up page after page until it was tiring. Then I'd start the next day, lying again. Pages of it. It broke the million mark on Amazon, meaning that a million other books sold more than it, but it finally settled into a nine-hundred-thousand number for about a week. Then more books came out, and it was back up there. It's called *Ruined Days* and it has eighteen five-star reviews. It maybe sold eighteen copies, unless some of those reviewers bought it used. The poetry books have not sold as well.

Then, I wrote a nonfiction book of essays. Pretty truthful, as I'm not running for office or anything where I have to be on my outwardly-good behavior. In fact, you're reading it, and I thank you!

I've just been notified that my adoption papers are coming through; I'm being adopted by Bernie Sanders. I wrote to him right before the DNC screwed up his first run for president and asked that he do this. I think he's a pretty nice person, and we'd probably get along. He also has this extra house on Lake Champlain where I could go to write. I could live there with my wife (not the first one) and my two—or is it three?—kids. Plenty of room, nice light, and the lake, of course. Other than loons, it's quiet, I imagine. Motorboats in summer maybe. He's so involved in politics and too busy to use even one home, and if he's elected by write-in he'll have to live in that D.C. swamp. Being newly adopted, he may want me to visit out there after the quarantine. I hope not. I think Bernie is rich. That would be great. It's what I always wanted in a parent. Don't forget to buy my books. That's it. I'm done for now. My pants are on fire.

TO LIVE AND DIE IN LA

THAT IS NOT too dramatic a title, actually. I did live in LA. And my life truly was in danger there, for a period of time. I worked at a very large advertising agency on a very large automotive account. Incidentally, one of the commercials we did was shot at the postmodern house featured in the movie *To Live and Die in L.A.* It was a concrete or stucco structure as I recall, and quite Bauhaus, perhaps straying into the territory of architectural Brutalism. But that's just a memory nudge for the title itself. Good film, by the way. One of the last good noir movies. A William Friedkin-directed film, it had a bitching car chase unlike any I'd previously seen—a wrong way on the freeway. An aerial view of that onrush of cars was breathtaking. They must have choreographed five hundred cars and drivers for that white-knuckle deal. It was a very good flick in 1985, and it stands up well over time.

Anyway, it started like this, the danger part. I rewrote another guy's copy. The Executive Creative Director requested it. I looked at the previous words, found them poetic but a bit florid, a little too dramatic for the car they described, rewrote same, put it in the system. This was back before the mass shootings became like bugs on a windshield

("Oh, there's another one."[5]): the last one I could recall was that spooky Texas tower shooting in 1966, and that was a hazy memory. At any rate, the guy whose copy I rewrote was heard to say something to the effect of, "The list of people who I'm gonna take out is growing." Then he appeared in my office (yes, we had offices then; the cubicle craze had not yet begun), wearing a black T-shirt with white letters proclaiming, KILL 'EM ALL, LET GOD SORT IT OUT. And it wasn't even casual Friday. He also sported cargo fatigues and mil-spec boots. I guess I was open-mouthed. I'd completely forgotten the rewrite and I didn't remember it then. I knew the guy, vaguely; it was a big agency. Let's call him Dave.

"Hi, Dave. What's up?"

"I brought you something." He reached behind his back, whipped out a knife in a scabbard, and handed it to me.

I took it, noting it had a plastic camo handle with a compass embedded in the top.

"Uhh. For me?"

"Yeah, it's a survival knife. I got it in Mexico." The agency was in Los Angeles County, a short drive from Mexico. People went there all the time. I removed the knife from the cheap sheath, saw that it had a serrated edge for ... cleaning fish? Opening oysters? It looked like the poorly-made stuff one picks up at a sale table in Juarez.

"You shouldn't have. A survival knife?"

"Yeah. Never know when you might need it."

"I shall treasure it."

---

5 Not to minimize these horrid shootings. Two more have just happened, one victimized Asian women in Georgia, the other, grocery shoppers in Colorado. I am not unmoved, simply numb. What does it take to keep assault weapons out of the hands of crazy people?

An awkward silence followed, me grinning maniacally and waving my new crappy knife in the air. Dave stood for a while, arms at his side so I could read his T-shirt, perhaps. Then my phone rang, and he was gone. I worked for an Executive Creative Director and a CD. I was a group CD. It was the ECD on the phone.

"Hey, G, could you come to my office?"

The ECD was from the Bronx, pretty straight-talking and somewhat bluff. After announcing that we had a "little staff problem," he asked me, "Did you tell Dave the writer to go fuck himself the other day? In the elevator?" After I protested such an unpleasant exchange, he said, "Oh I don't mind if you did, he probably deserved it, but if you didn't, then he's having hallucinations, or worse. He's compiling scores to settle."

"Why would he do that?"

"It's complicated. In any case, I ask that you avoid him or treat him with kid gloves for a while."

"Okay." Then I told him about the survival knife and the odd conversation in my office and we ended the topic—he on a worried note. I won't say I didn't think about the situation, but it took a back seat as other problems pushed it from the forefront.

Perhaps a week later, in the elevator, a scene took place that imprinted on my memory screen firmly enough to pop up vividly even today, years later. It was near lunchtime. The only other occupant in the elevator was a young woman who worked at the agency in a secretarial or production capacity; I'd seen her around. No cellphones back then or we'd each have been gazing at one, mouth breathing. I smiled and nodded. She moved next to me, into "my space." The eye contact that had begun with acknowledgment intensified. Then she did something that still elicits goosebumps; I was wearing a polo shirt, and she touched my bare arm with the back of an index finger grazing it from inner elbow to wrist and back again. While locking eyes and dimpling just a little with a slight smile. Not a word. It was quite overtly sexy. The door opened on the ground floor, and she walked out. I think I was frozen there for an instant and had to stop the door from closing by leaving. No sign of her in the hall. I proceeded out the front door and into the bright California sunlight. The incident would have registered firmly even if she hadn't been someone who I knew by happenstance that Dave was pursuing ardently.

Habitually, I arrived at work by five a.m. Few were around at that time, but I saw Dave with a large batch of flowers one of those early mornings and, while I was starting the coffee machines on another floor, I saw him lay the bouquet down on the elevator lady's desk in a secretarial or accounting area that had some desks laid out in a communal arrangement.

So, here I was in some kind of unanticipated, unwanted love triangle. I couldn't laugh it off; the elevator incident had been too pointed, too explicit to be anything but a come-on. Not that she wasn't attractive, but if Dave was dogging her tracks I wanted well away from the both of them.

A few days later, I was pacing the Creative Floor hallway, my wont when thinking, and I saw a new guy in an office near the ECD's office. I was usually apprised of new arrivals, so this was unusual. I asked the CD who the new guy was. The CD, also from New York, like the ECD, and very forthcoming in a humorous way, was oddly evasive. "He's a special projects guy. He's just here to work with the ECD. Secret stuff."

Secret stuff. Very unlike the creative department. We were an open bunch and practiced complementarity, having discovered creativity flourished in such an atmosphere. I stopped by the new man's office and introduced myself. He seemed flustered when I told him what I worked on and offered assistance in finding needed materials, or introductions, whatever he might find helpful in negotiating the system in his first few days. Usually, there was an orientation period during which the FNG got paraded around, met the folks, traded lies about awards and accounts, and settled into whatever group he or she was hired to work with, or for, or over.

This new guy was young, had a very heavy German accent, and acted like he was totally unsuited for the louche behavior on the creative floor.

"What's with the new guy? Really?" I asked my immediate boss.

Rich was a very humorous and outspoken Italian from New York. His answer was hesitant and without his usual disarming wit. "You can't repeat this," he said. "The new guy is a bodyguard."

"No shit? For who?" I knew in a flash it was true. The German guy was in good shape and moved like a cat, nervous as he was. It turned out, he was there to provide protection for the executive creative director and was positioned down the hall and at an angle to the ECD's corner office that would allow for easy viewing and quick access. Rich's office was at the opposite corner, and mine was somewhere in-between.

Rich and the ECD were on Dave's shit list, as was I. An informant had given them the list of about twenty names that Dave had said he was "taking with him when he went out." All the names had been guilty of a real or imagined slight. Dave's therapist had either finally called or had someone call the agency about Dave's attempt to buy a gun.

The gun dealer had balked because he felt Dave was either drunk or on drugs and had informed the police. Somehow the therapist had been questioned and public safety won out over doctor/patient confidentiality.

Rich got up and shut his office door, then he reached into a balled-up suede jacket lying on his desk and pulled out a shiny nickel-plated .45 semi-automatic. He made several quick moves like the TV detectives do, whirling about, gun held in both hands.

"Shit!" I ducked reflexively.

"In case the German guy isn't fast enough." Rich grinned evilly.

"Is that thing loaded?"

"All guns are loaded." He handed it to me, grip first, after sliding the action back, ejecting a shell. It was a heavy piece, Desert Eagle.

"Paisano with a big Hebrew cannon—don't fuck with me," he said, pulling a face that was usually followed by his explosive, contagious laugh.

He took the thing with him when we went to lunch, pulled it in the parking lot, and we dodged between cars in a parody of *Miami Vice*. I'll always remember that scene, giddy and laughing, ducking and whirling behind cars; unfortunately, Rich, still a young man, died of a heart attack within two years of that strange time.

Sadly, the ECD also passed away, but at a more advanced age and at his retirement choice of Shelter Island, New York. But while he was hale, hearty, alive, and attempting to stay that way, he added me to the list of the in-house protectorate. So, I was on two lists now. The German guy was friendlier, and he patrolled, watched, and noted times of exit and entrance. I suppose he was armed.

My habit was to arrive at work at about five a.m., the same time as the brokers on the first floor. They had to respond to New York time, which was three hours later. I would take the elevator to the seventh floor, make coffee, and settle in for my day; I preferred the silence for my first few hours of work. The thing was: Dave began lurking about early as well. We had every right to be there, ostensibly, but seeing flashes of a person who had vowed to take me with him on his possible day of exit spooked the hell out of me.

"I wanted to show you something I wrote, see if it measures up to your high standards."

The voice was behind me. I hadn't heard Dave enter my office. I think I uttered something like "Aiiiiieeeeyahh!" loudly, as I tried to keep from falling out of my chair. The clock said six in the morning. Daylight was rising pinkish through the mist outside my windows. And there stood Dave, too close, holding a sheet of typewritten copy. It was a love letter to the elevator lady.

"Uhh, Dave, maybe it's not, ahh, appropriate for me to read this. I mean, you know, it's ...

personal ..." I trailed off.

"It would mean a lot, your opinion." He stood, weight on one foot as though ready to spring.

Keeping him in my peripheral vision I read it. Schmaltzy, heart-to-heart, let's get it on stuff. "Well, it should get her attention, Dave. I can only assume you know her pretty well?"

"Well enough." He smiled, conspiratorially.

"Then let 'er fly, I'd say. Faint heart ne'er won fair lady."

"Give you a tip. Next time you're going under for plunder, use a Wint-O-Green lifesaver. Better yet a menthol cough drop. Drives 'em nuts."

"Thanks, Dave. Well, back to work ..." I waggled my fingers at the keyboard like an eager pianist. When I looked back around, he was gone. I tried to dim the image in my mind of Dave and the elevator lady, as he pops a mint in his mouth and hits the deck. But then, if they got together that would seem to sap energy from other endeavors, such as blowing my head off in the early hours and lying in wait for others on his list. The German guy arrived at nine with the majority of the creatives. Maybe I would change my hours as well.

I envisioned Dave asking Elevator Lady, "Going down?" That made me laugh out loud as I typed. I was becoming giddy and weird with the strange atmospherics swirling about. I had questions: Why didn't they just lay him off? Or maybe have him committed?

The constant state of menace was tiring and I was becoming paranoid; at home, I was hearing noises that were new to me. The outside stairs leading up to my door sounded off when someone hurried up or down them; the previous night, someone had bounded up them and down again. It had been the pizza guy discovering he was at the wrong door. The townhouse was two separate residences and had a front and a back entrance, A and B. I was B and more secluded.

Another sound I noticed more and more was that of the free-range peacocks of Palos Verdes. A thing there for some reason—they wandered everywhere. They screeched and sometimes made noises like a cat yowling or a child hollering No! That was eroding what peace of mind I had left.

The next day I was at work, and about 7:30 a.m. I was standing out by the coffee machines getting a refill when something shiny and hard bounced off my shoulder. I whirled around, spilling hot coffee on my arm. "Dammit!" I dropped the Styrofoam cup, bent to pick up the shiny object, and I felt my whole center of balance go. Earthquake, I realized.

More shiny objects fell from the ceiling; they were chrome sprinkler casings. Drawers slid open beneath the coffee machines. Drawers of filing cabinets in the hallway screeched open. The building yawed. I went to look out the windows upon what appeared to be a normal sunny day, blue sky, birds flying, traffic moving. I decided to get the hell out before an aftershock hit; this was the seventh floor ,and I did what I normally do: hit the button on the elevator. Wrong. You are warned not to take elevators during an earthquake.

I remembered this while descending and duly noted the swing of the elevator as it bumped things on the way down. I got to the ground floor and saw Dave flitting around a column. Or was I imagining that? No matter. If I lived long enough, I was making some calls today and getting out. Yes, it was Dave. He flitted behind another column. Where was that German guy when you needed him, anyway? Outside, the brokers' vehicles and my own howled like an air raid in WWII England, all the car alarms in arrhythmic discord. The light poles swayed as an aftershock rolled through. The brokers' cars, a Maserati among them, wailed anew. Mine too: a GMC truck that would become more and more appropriate as the miles spooled out behind me on the way back to Kansas. If I lived long enough. To live and die in LA was a movie title. You can't go home, of course; the concept *home* wasn't there anymore, and I was cagey enough to know it. *Home* was Christmases, high school, first marriages, dogs and horses, and yearnings. *Home* was "Moon River," vanished people, a Schwinn bike, and the first pay envelope. Home was people who loved you or didn't, and all of them were gone.

Dave appeared in front of me in his "LET GOD SORT IT OUT" T-shirt. "You looked like you were surfing in the parking lot. Funny." Then he popped a mint into his mouth, winked, and headed back into the building. The parking lot rippled a bit and, sure enough, I spread my arms for balance.

In a day, I had another job, gave two-weeks notice, directed a moving company to load up some furniture and the Harley, invoked my last month's rent on the townhouse, laid low by changing my hours around, and never saw Dave or LA again. There was no mass shooting. Dave had been a mechanism, like an earthquake or other sudden realization that it was time to go. Simply that. California Dreamin' was no longer viable.

Joan Didion said, in "Notes from a Native Daughter:" "California is a place in which a boom mentality and a sense of Chekhovian loss meet in uneasy suspension; in which the mind is troubled by some buried but ineradicable suspicion that things had better work here, because here, beneath that immense bleached sky, is where we run out of continent."

Things *had* worked here. I'd just taken it as far as I could. The next thing was Australia or back where I came from. Back I went. Sometimes that, Messrs. Wolfe and Alger, is where you go, and it takes every bit as much moxie, if not more, than forging ever west or seeking something where *home* used to be.

I wish I could give the reader closure on the Dave thing. As for myself, I guess I don't need it. Curiosity has compelled me to ask a couple of Los Angeles people who were somewhat familiar with that time, but they knew nothing. The ones closest to it have passed away, perhaps Dave, too. I looked online for his obituary but found nothing, not even his name in any search; it's as though he disappeared or never existed. Usually, writers will eventually come up with a book or a screenplay, but not Dave, apparently. Nothing on Amazon or IMDb, not even a Facebook page. He'd mentioned a title of a movie he was thinking about, a macabre film about a poetic serial killer, *No Rhyme, No Reason.*

I think of that time as the mass shooting that never occurred. There were twenty on his list and it was growing daily. His therapist was alarmed enough to alert the office and a gun store in Torrance, which then refused his purchase of a semi-automatic weapon by saying it was probably just a glitch and to try back later. But the agency had been told of the list previously by a coworker who he'd confided in early on in this drama. While Dave never got his plan off the ground, the decade exploded into mass shootings; while the seventies listed fifteen such events (among those was Kent State) and seventy-six dead, the eighties list was close to 200. And, sadly, we're aware of the decades' tolls since. The elimination of bump stocks and extra-capacity magazines seems like a bad joke in *The Onion*. I have no stance, no soapbox, but I might feel very different had I gone to work one day and caught a .223 in the shoulder and lived through the terror. *To Live and Die in L.A.* Good movie. Not a great life plan. For me, anyway.

MY OWN SMALL ADMISSIONS SCANDAL

THE SATs WERE around when I was of an age to take the test, but I don't remember doing it. Why should I take such a test when I had no desire to attend college? My high-school grades were room temperature, though an English teacher had threatened to put me into advanced English at one point. I didn't need that. I had a girlfriend, a hot rod, a job; things were going nicely.

You know those writers who proudly proclaim to be the first in their family to attend college? They *should* be proud; I'm not denigrating them. But I would be the first in my family *not* to attend college if I had my way. I wasn't to have my way. I didn't know the main reason my folks wanted me to attend a college of my or their choice was to get me the hell out of the house. It had worked with my sister. She'd gone to OU back when we'd lived in Tulsa. Then she became an airline hostess for Braniff. Then she'd gotten married. All nicely out-of-house. Her grades were worse than mine.

I recall my stepfather saying, "You can go to any school you want. Name it."

"Princeton," I said. A friend and I joked around that we should go there on the basis of the haircut. We'd seen a picture of "The Princeton" at the barbershop where we got our ducktails trimmed.

"I'm not sure your grades would support that choice, Butch." He looked worried.

Had he been wealthy, it still would not have been a possibility. Had I been a rocket scientist and gone to M.I.T. or some prestigious college, he may have felt some pride. Most likely not. Nor was my mother any Felicity Huffman. (Who, to be fair, probably just wanted the best for her daughter.) My parents were greasing the skids, not trying to get me on a rowing team through some duplicitous admissions coach so they could tell their friends their kid had just been admitted to *Cool Name University*.

A Netflix documentary tells me that some people pay half a million for this ... privilege. Or more! Those people must have way, way, *waaayyyy* too much money. And inverse social insecurity. If I had that much money I might get a street-legal McLaren, and the kids could go to JC or State, whatever might let them in.

At any rate, my mother's cousin was admissions counselor at a small Midwestern college and I'm guessing she pulled that string. I got in. The folks moved. I stayed in the "guest bedroom" that Christmas and noted the new house was exorcised of any sign of me and my sister other than the requisite cute little kid snapshot.

When Joan Didion failed to be admitted to Stanford, her first choice of two, she was horrified, then heartbroken. All of her friends who had applied there had been accepted. Her parents were not invested in her colleges of choice. In "Let me Tell You What I Mean," she says, "Their idea of their own worth and of my worth remained independent of where, or even if, I went to college." And her father simply shrugged and offered her a drink.

Anyway, I attended several colleges with nary a bribe. And I worked to help out with tuition and bills. Filling stations, a coffee shop/gallery, the school cafeteria, nights at a mortuary, tending bar when I turned twenty-one. And my folks thanked me for all of that. And I got better at school. Maybe I grew up a bit and did some grappling with reality. Off and on. It's not a contest I relish.

And I've come to find that life itself is an admissions process. Many apply, few are chosen. And some of us are rejected daily, regularly. They call us writers.

TRINITY

TRINITY. A code word for a part of the Manhattan Project and also for the unity of The Father, The Son, and The Holy Ghost. As a child, I learned about the latter Trinity in an amalgam of the Catholic Church and the Episcopal Church.

My dad was Catholic. My mother had just married an Episcopalian, my stepfather. He worked on the Manhattan Project, but I didn't know that until later. It was wartime. World War Two and I was a little boy who spent a lot of time visiting or living with various grandparents. Three sets of them. My mother and stepfather were off and running. "Traipsing," as one grandparent put it.

I'll call him The Atomic Guy. Sometimes, he was at Oak Ridge and other times he was at Los Alamos. She was with him a lot, and those had to be pretty exciting times. I know they were in Reno from the red dice and ashtrays I saw. That's probably where she divorced my dad. Whatever they did, wherever they went, they didn't have to explain anything to anyone. It was all secret. Top Secret. I imagine that added some spice to the traipsing. I recall, quite clearly, a fringed, bright red buckskin jacket my mother wore in those days. Bucking broncs were embroidered on it. Saguaro cactus. It was the sort of go-to-hell statement people made back then. She had a bag to match. The Atomic Guy wore cowboy boots.

Every year, and there have been a lot of them, as the long hot summer nears my birthday in August, the whole Atomic Bomb thing rears its death's head. It's time for The Media to drum up anniversary articles about nukes in general and, at this time of year, the specific war-ender, the last word being key. It did end the war, after all. At horrific human cost. But not ours, not this time. War *is* hell as The Greatest Generation discovered, and as our own hawkish last few administrations should know but act like it's a requirement of government. Few recall how close the Nazis were to their own *totenkopf bombe,* and they would have pulled out all the stops to use it. We got there first. And, in any case, The Reich got thoroughly vanquished by May of 1945. A few months later we exploded Pandora's Box to hell and gone. We had to.

August 6, 1945: the U.S. dropped Little Boy on Hiroshima. Then, on August 9: we bombed Nagasaki with Fat Man. A third bombing planned for August 19, according to declassified documents, another Fat Man, became unnecessary. The location for that bombing is unknown. But that wasn't to be the end of it. Not by a long shot. As many as *seven more bombs* (on the order of Fat Man) were in the pipeline to be used by the end of October, had the Japanese not surrendered.

August 12, 1945: I celebrated my seventh birthday, blissfully unaware that children my age had been imprinted on floors of leveled buildings in Japan. Nor did I know the physical weight of Little Boy. The plane, *Enola Gay,* jumped ten feet after dropping the innocuously-named load. Let that sink in. I know many things about those days now. I read a lot.

Fifty years ago, in the basement of my folks' house, while looking through file cabinets for a birth certificate for passport purposes, I came upon a polished wood plaque. Twenty-two names on it. One of the names was that of my stepfather. The inscription above the names thanked the list for their part in "the surrender of Japan in WWII," and the signature was, I believe, that of Harry Truman. Of course, it was not his real signature; it was all embossed and, probably, state-of-the-art plaque-wise; today, it would have been polished steel or chrome with Plexiglas. After my mother died, my stepfather remarried and I imagine the plaque found its way to eBay or some such place. I won't go into what became of the considerable fortune he'd amassed, some of it my mother's inheritance.

Back in the 1950s, I began to notice that my stepfather became a morose drunk around the time of my birthday. It was unusual for him to get so blotto back then. I sometimes saw it as a sort of humanity trying to submerge the horror of the event, but that wars with another strong thought; that he was beginning to see, in the day-to-day, that there would never again be as exhilarating a time as there was in the all-out race of the Manhattan Project, a marathon for which he was uniquely suited. Never would he feel so expressly alive and ... necessary. This is the thought that wins, knowing him as I did. His arrogance may have come from entering college at fifteen with a stratospheric IQ compared to his teen peers. And a rebelliousness against goody-goodness and his father, an Episcopal minister.

He once told me an overkill story about shooting ducks in Delaware from a yacht of some kind; the ducks came in waves and he and his friends kept killing them. Retrieved with small boats, they hung them from the rails on the sides of the big boat until there was nowhere else to hang them, so they piled them on the deck. The point of the story, if there was one, was lost on me. The killing, the marksmanship, seemed to be the essence here, the admirable thing. I didn't ask what happened to the bounty, but I should have. I know the hunters sailed into port triumphantly laden with ducks and proud to show them. I was, by no means, a conservationist when told about this, but I registered a sort of puzzled shame, a bit of heat in my face. I still do when this floats to my consciousness. But *WTF* is my thought now.

He taught me to hunt, where the safety was on the Ithaca 16-gauge pump he gave me when I turned twelve. How to lead a pheasant or a duck. How to get through a barbed-wire fence with a gun safely. How to shoot in your zone, and into a sky situation. Never command another man's bird dog, etc.

Sometime in my twenties, he asked for the gun back, to give to a friend's son, I think. He said, "You know, that Ithaca pump I lent you." I said I'd look for it. Of course, around the atomic anniversary and my birthday he was tanked again; he forgot giving it to me with a "You're old enough, now, Butch ..." speech. It still hangs in a gun rack at the farm today, unused for sixty years. I quit hunting one day in Nebraska and never went back. I still walked the fields. That was the part I liked. When he died, I got a Remington 12-gauge, nothing more. I hadn't expected even the gun. Another *WTF* thought. Or, is this a joke?

We lived in Tulsa when I was twelve. The Atomic Guy now worked in the oil business, an electrical engineer. Suddenly, we were speaking Spanish as much as possible as a family, trying to learn the language as we were anticipating a move to Caracas, Venezuela. I recall hearing "Rum and Coca-Cola (Working for the Yankee dollar)" at high volume at house parties, the rugs rolled back for dancing. I think they were trying to recreate that old wartime frenzy and no-tomorrow atmosphere. I thought it was fine. I was given orange-juice glasses of beer and got into the spirit, presaging my own battle with booze to come. We moved back to Kansas City rather than Venezuela. As a teen entering high school, it was just as strange a move to me. After attending a dozen grade schools, the Tulsa interlude had been a relatively stable few years.

I've said nothing of my biological dad here; that's another story, and he deserves much more space than this one will provide. He came home from service as a radioman on a ship, in a sailor suit. I dug the look. He was a good, kind man. A sharp dresser, he worked in haberdashery for a while, then settled into a government job in air traffic control which he despised until the day he finally retired. I know that he identified with a Robert Service poem, "The Men That Don't Fit In," much like so many who returned from the war in the Forties and found assimilation to the boom-time fifties confusing and alien; not to mention PTSD, of which nothing was known at the time. The overall feeling was something described by Hunter S. Thompson, or at least ascribed to him, years later, as: "All my life, my heart has sought a thing I cannot name." I know my dad would agree. I know I get it. He puttered with radios a while, some kit he sent for on the back of a matchbook cover. It didn't take. He taught me some Morse Code on a telegraph key he had. S.O.S. for one thing. Dit dit dit, dah dah dah, dit dit dit. Nobody came to save us. He had gone to college at Creighton and was captain of the track team, a dash man. His time in the one-hundred-yard dash was 0.01 off of Jesse Owens' time. He quit college and track, abruptly. No explanation.

Trinity. The first (but waaayyy short of the last) test of a radioactive bomb. Alamogordo. The Atomic Guy may or may not have been there. He was in New Mexico in those days. The story is J. Robert Oppenheimer named the first tested bomb Trinity because of a John Donne poem he admired. The poem has nothing to do with trinity. Another Donne poem barely touches on the Holy Trinity by mentioning "the three-personned God." Anyway, what's in a name? The globelike device was called "Gadget." They set it off at Jornada Del Muerto. There's a name for you; it translates to English, roughly, as Journey of the Dead

The blast produced the infamous mushroom cloud that ascended to 38,000 feet. The thing was a stupendous and fiery success that elicited a quote from the well-read Oppenheimer from the Bhagavad-Gita, a long line that ended in, "Now I become Death, the destroyer of worlds." Kenneth Bainbridge, the test director, was more plain-spoken: "Now we are all sons of bitches." But all of this is known and reiterated in August: the tons of TNT equivalencies, the awe, the brightness and heat, the kayoing thump for miles—it's all, at last, indescribable in human terms. May the Father and The Son and The Holy Ghost protect us all. Amen.

There were no evacuations. It was a secret of the highest order, so no one was warned. People died from the long-term effects. Cows ate contaminated grass while radioactive ash settled on their backs. People ate the cows. Drank the milk. Some looked directly at the fireball and lost their sight for a time, some seeing only in a reverse-negative-tintype sort of visualizing for days, weeks, never to fully regain the sight they'd had before. Stories abound. Official and unofficial. New ones will surface. We can't get enough of the horror. The tests continued, as we know, after the war—let the ashes fall where they may.

Picture this: The Atomic Guy and my mother in her red-fringed buckskin. They are sitting on the hood of Liberace's pink Cadillac convertible in the desert near Las Vegas. It is just before dawn, and they are being served mimosas. I don't know how this dreamlike diorama came about, but I know it did. I was told about it. They are there to witness a nuclear test north of Las Vegas. They are allowed closer than most tourists, due to some finagling. The Atomic Guy lights a cigarette with a flourish of his Zippo, clacks it shut. He says, "Watch this. Nothing like it." He is living an American Dream of Victory. Necessity. Do or die. For some reason, the soundtrack in my head is The Chordettes' "Mr. Sandman."

OFF TRACK–WHAT I DID WITH ONE HUNDRED DOLLARS

WARNING: I'll tell you right up front, I booby-trapped this rather meandering essay with a silly Broadway tune that, once absorbed into your already crowded headspace, will remain there to annoy you for a long, *long* time. Maybe always. I still haven't gotten rid of it. When I wrote this piece, I had to look up a book or two that I had read on horserace handicapping to get the authors' names right and during the search, there it was. *I Got the Horse Right Here: Damon Runyon on Horse Racing*

Something clicked into place when I saw that title, something from many years ago. I'm not a Broadway-tune guy, though I've been known to break into a phony basso profondo of "Ooooooo-klahoma, where the wind comes sweepin' down the plain ..." if I'm sure I'm alone. Maybe the dogs get treated to this on a pasture and woods walk. They know me for the total nerd that I am and love me despite my uncoolness. Dogs don't care.

What clicked: Damon Runyon + *Guys and Dolls* + a song I thought I'd forgotten but like a chicken pox virus, had lain in wait. It's a song that crawls into you and grows. In you not on you. Much more benign than COVID, you're still the host to something, if not malarial, that's as hard to shake. Thank Frank Loesser.

I got the horse right here,
The name is Paul Revere,
And here's a guy that says if the weather's clear,
Can do,
Can do,
This guy says the horse can do,

and so on and on and on in a bunch more verses and can-do's, without drawing an apparent breath in its falling gracefully down the stairs catchiness. Got it? I will proceed with my tale.

I'm not a gambler; not a good one anyway. My Uncle Pete was. Reno Pete. My earliest recollection of Pete was him pouring concrete splash blocks for gutter drains and stacking them on a flatbed truck at my grandmother's. It was not a rural setting. This was Mr. and Mrs. Bridge territory over by Ward Parkway in Kansas City. A short walk to the spectacular Rose Garden in Jacob L. Loose Park or a stroll past the Russell Stover manse. His enterprise was not looked upon with favor by neighbors.

Pete used part of a vacant lot next door to form and pour these things. Then, when they set up, he'd take them out of the form and pour some more. My guess is he'd talked his folks (my maternal grandparents) into using their backyard and vacant lot to start a business. Their yardman didn't like it, not one bit. The mixing mess and the cement dust interfered with his plans. The yardman's name was Ras (pronounced Ross), and the story was he was a displaced Arabian prince. I believed it. I was maybe ten and thought it a marvelous story, that my grandparents' lawn was watched over by Arabian royalty; of course, Ali Baba and Aladdin books entered into my thinking.

Pete and Ras got into it, verbally, and I was crestfallen; two of my favorite people were at odds and both had solid arguments to back up their angry words. I put my hands to my ears and ran to the below-ground garage with Rusty, the old Cocker Spaniel, who also preferred a more peaceful atmosphere. The driveway wound around behind the house and led down to the large garage. It was a wonderful-smelling cavern of oils, gasoline, and cleaning fluids; it was Ras's HQ as he did several properties in the neighborhood and he kept his equipment here: push mowers, shrub clippers, grass whips, and the like. It also housed my grandfather's black Lincoln Zephyr. This was maybe 1948. Things seemed simpler then. It wasn't Ras's wrath that made Pete reconsider the splash block business. My educated guess is Pete encountered a poor effort-to-dollar ratio. Shortly after this, he became a full-time gambler: horses his specialty, poker and craps, his job diversions.

Pete was never lazy. After his stint in the Army Air Corps, he'd helped build airstrips in Tangier, Morocco and other far-flung places in the hegemonic race for post-war territorial advantage. He'd worked in the oil fields and was a roughneck in the crew that brought in the largest gusher in the world at that time in Louisiana, an H. L. Hunt enterprise. He'd raced motorcycles on flat tracks and done well at it. But he had a head for figures, honed at The Colorado School of Mines, and that came together with a love for horse racing. Pete told me he had a "system." He became a handicapper, keeping dry and muddy track statistics, speed ratings, owners, trainers, jockeys, last and recent wins, and he bet accordingly. He made a living at it. Of course, no successful handicapper relies solely on a system—gut instinct is part of it. As Ted McClelland points out in *Horseplayers, Life at the Track,* "It has to be developed by watching thousands of races and losing thousands of dollars until, eventually, you have a feel for the tote board, the way a guitarist has a feel for the next note, the way a carpenter has a feel for just how hard he should press his chisel against the lathe to winnow a perfect table leg." Pete had that innate skill and, against all odds, he made a living at the track, mainly Caliente in Tijuana. He finally moved and lived there the last thirty years of his life. Pissed off at a DUI he got in San Diego, he told me, "A sawbuck to the officer in Tijuana and you're on your way again."

My nickname back then was Butch, and a girl I knew from Little Rock had bet on a horse named Butch's Dream at Oaklawn in Hot Springs, Arkansas. Pete was in town about then, and I asked him if he knew the horse. He consulted a well-worn leather notebook and read me the stats. Stride on turf. Stride on dirt. Race lengths the horse liked. Muddy or dry. All sorts of info. Clearly, Pete had found his métier.

When Derby Day rolls around I always get a little quickening of the senses; my folks used to have Derby parties, and one year Pete was there. He took bets from those who wanted to wager, passed them along to his bookie. There was no off-track betting at the time, no legal OTB. Pete was usually at the big-stakes races. I still have a win ticket from Churchill Downs in 1955 that Pete got signed by Diamond Jim Moran. They used to pay British royalty $10,000 to attend the Derby—Moran got $50,000. Runyonesque. (*I got the horse right here ...*)

I think of Pete as Derby Day nears and the last few years I've won hypothetical money on win bets, trifectas, and some admittedly wuss across the board bets. Then I would ignore the Preakness and Belmont Stakes other than to see if there was a Triple Crown winner.

This year I decided to put some money on the three races, or at least the first one if I lost it all on The Derby. Minimal research guided me to an online betting resource with a good reputation. They offered a one-hundred-dollar sign-up bonus, but I bypassed that, suspecting strings, and put one hundred dollars of my own into my betting balance: half for me, half for my wife. Then I began checking out the probable Derby horses, their trainers, jockeys, past races, and weather forecasts for Churchill Downs. I did a bunch of work leading up to the race and on Derby Day I bet some exactas and one or two longer-odds horses. I also placed some across the board bets. My wife? She picked a Baffert and a Pletcher, money on the nose and to place. "I don't go for all that exotic stuff," she said, "all those triplectas or whatever." She won. I mainly lost, except for a place bet on Hot Rod Charlie in an across-the- board bet. She had Medina Spirit at 12-1 to win and Mandaloun to win, place, or show. So we had about eighty bucks to wager on the Preakness, thanks to her.

My wife had lost interest in the other races, so I doubled down on my latent handicapping knowledge gleaned one season at Omaha's Ak-Sar-Ben Track and Coliseum, a track so iffy it wasn't even listed in Las Vegas. This was in the sixties. Back then, I was a field engineer for a paving company and spent all my days outdoors at various jobs figuring the yield on concrete pours. I also spent time at

Ak-Sar-Ben, as did some of my colleagues. To make that season-long story shorter, I did a lot of figuring, slide-rule work, and hand-calculator figures, filling yellow-lined pads with figures. At the end of the season I was ahead twelve dollars. That was because, on the last day, a field superintendent told me to bet Wise Boots to win. He was connected, so I did. Ten bucks to win. Wise Boots ran at 8-1 and my thought as he crossed the wire five lengths ahead of the closest horse, was: *Why didn't I bet one hundred dollars?* Because I didn't have it; one hundred dollars back then was like $1,000 now. But the horse covered some losses. I never placed another (horse) bet.

Until the 2021 Derby. That atavistic Reno Pete gene surfaced and Hot Rod Charlie called to me. I bet him to win. Later, he looked even better when Baffert's horses were pulled, in a controversial decision by the racing officials, moving Pletcher up a notch to winner and Hot Rod Charlie to third, or show position. But Hot Rod Charlie was not to run in the Preakness. That race sneaked up on me anyway. Unprepared, I bet feebly. Low-odds horses that ran at even lower odds. One or two silly bets. I came out less than even and vowed to up the ante in the Belmont Stakes. Of the original hundred, I was down to about fifty dollars.

As Belmont neared I did some homework. Only eight horses were running, Hot Rod Charlie among them. (*I got the horse right here ...*) The longest odds horse at 30-1 was France Go de Ina, the Japanese entry. Belmont was offering Japanese entries a million dollars more if one of theirs won. So the incentive was there, and I reasoned that they wouldn't have brought a horse all the way over if they didn't think they had a chance at it. This awkwardly-named horse was a beauty, and I was drawn to the three-year-old chestnut, even though he'd "thrown" an exercise rider in May. I looked up this particular workout and viewed it several times. It looked to me as though the rider stepped off the horse. But what do I know? Maybe it was a workman's comp deal. Anyway, I was pretty thorough in checking all eight contenders' last few wins, losses, and Beyer Speed Figures, and wouldn't have bet the race had it been, say, at Ak-Sar-Ben years before. But I was determined to bet the Triple Crown, whoever was running.

History, you old teacher, you. I did bet Ten across the board on France GDI for thirty dollars. Bye bye, thirty dollars. France ran dead last. No one paid jack.

	Horse	Win	Place	Show
1	Essential Quality	$4.60	$3.00	$2.60
2	Hot Rod Charlie		$4.10	$2.90
3	Rombauer			$3.50
4	Known Agenda			
5	Bourbonic			
6	Rock Your World			
7	Overtook			
8	France Go de Ina	(Or France Went de Ina)		

The win/place/show horses' numbers (not their finishing place numbers, but their jockey silks' numbers) were Essential Quality 2, Hot Rod Charlie 4, and Rombauer 3. And, I had bet some trifectas. 2-3-4 for six dollars. 4-3-2 for six dollars. and 2-4-3 for six dollars. Or so I thought. When I looked up my $200+ "winnings," I was dismayed to see I had only a $17.50 balance. Then I retraced my bets. Instead of betting 2-4-3, I had bet 4-3-2 twice. My fault. I meant to bet 2-4-3 but screwed up. Coulda, woulda, shoulda is the *bête noire* of bettors; so is: "Thought I did, coulda sworn ..."

So now, I have that sad balance of $17.50 in my off-track account. I waited until I finished this essay to blow it, so you will know the end result of my hundred bucks when I do. Logging on, I see a race at Churchill Downs in nineteen minutes to post. I see only one trainer name I recognize: Asmussen. It's an allowance race (usually broken maiden but not ready for stakes), and the horse's name is Excession. Ricardo Santana Jr. is the jockey, speed number is eighty-seven, up there with the favorites. Boom. Five dollars across the board for fifteen dollars of the $17.50. Six minutes to post. Leaves me a two-dollar bet. Let's see what happens. He's number six in the gate.

Oops, I did it again. I have this problem with numbers. In my haste I bet number four, a horse named Gigging. Saez up. Cano, trainer. Odds: 11-1. Just went to thirteen. Now at twelve. Someone likes him. Same speed numbers as Excession.

Results: neither Excession nor Gigging in the money. Here goes nothing. Or rather here goes my last two bucks. Churchill Downs again. Novel Squall to win. (I saw a race with Novel Squall, Oaklawn, where she was last, took the rail in a tight position, and won. A big wow, that race. No time to research; post is ten minutes. Novel Squall is the long odds at fourteen. Two dollars to win. Hey, this could get me back in the game. Come on, One! (This time I'm betting the horse's actual number instead of the profit line odds (nine). Now she's at 10-1. 9-1. Eight. Jeez, lots of folks betting her. Four minutes to go. Back up to 10-1. Tip sheet says, "clocker special." (Fast workout in the last few days.) She's in the rail position to start and liked the rail in that Oaklawn win. They're off!

Novel Squall ran third, but heckuva try. Good race actually. So this essay cost me $99.50 and didn't cost you a cent. Guess who the real winner is here.

Uncle Pete, where is that handicapping DNA when I need it? But I'll always have ... the horse right here. His name is Paul Revere. And there's a guy who says if the weather's clear ...

Now for the lyrics you'll never forget; if you're brave enough, go to Youtube and type in "Fugue for Tinhorns," *Guys and Dolls* (1955). And remember I warned you. But the lyrics should get an Oscar all by themselves.

ACKNOWLEDGEMENTS

"Writing Women: How I Do It" appeared in *Fiction Southeast*

"Chickens One Day, Feathers the Next" appeared in *Guttural Magazine*

"The Horse Worrier" appeared in *Roll*, an anthology

"Rejections: Bugs on the Windshield" appeared in *Bird's Thumb, Write Here Write Now*

"The Mangled Emmy" (originally "An Emmy is an Emmy is an Emmy") was a post for *Stage 32 Film Blog*

"They're Still Stealing van Goghs" appeared in the anthology *Resurrection of a Sunflower*

"Racism by Default" appeared in *The Good Men Project*

"Why I Write" appeared in *1888 Literary Center*

"The Unnaturalist" and "Knucklehead" appeared in *Stymie Magazine, A Journal of Sport, Games & Literature*

"A Tulsa Kind of Day" appeared in *Wild Word Magazine* (Berlin)

"Visualizing; Not a Woo Woo Science" and "To Live and Die in L.A." appeared in *Eclectica Magazine*

"Ioway Plates" appeared in *Sisyphus* (Hip Pocket Press)

"Ernest Thompson Seton, Malcolm X, and Me" appeared in *Sunspot Literary Journal*

"Truckers, Earn While You Learn" appeared in *Potato Soup Journal*

"Welterweights" appeared in *Wilderness House Literary Review*

"Ski. If you can. All you can." appeared in *Ski Journal*

"I Always Wanted a Junkyard" appeared in *Sandy River Review*

"George Lois Made Me Do It" appeared in *Meat for Tea: The Valley Review*

"Rocky and the Rebel Punk" appeared in *Wordrunner* Spring 2020 anthology

"Covid Days, Chocolate Nights" appeared in *Litro Magazine* (UK)

"Forget it Jake. It's Hollywood. A Review," appeared in *LitBreak Magazine*

"Thoughts that came in unbidden from the clouds while mowing pasture and spoken into a small recorder" appeared in *Jellyfish Review*

"Just for the Love of It" and "Make Me an Angel" appeared in *Blue Mountain Review*

"Lying for Fun and Profit" appeared in *The Daily Drunk*

"Come Together. Right Now." appeared in *Nobody's Home Anthology of Modern Southern Folklore*

"Trinity" appeared in *Drunk Monkeys Review*

"Off Track (What I Did with One Hundred Dollars)" appeared in *Big City Lit*

OTHER BOOKS BY THIS AUTHOR

I Was in the Vicinity
Horses See Ghosts
Scattered Cranes
Ruined Days
Resume Speed
Night Train, Cold Beer

VINE LEAVES PRESS

Enjoyed this book?
Go to *vineleavespress.com* to find more.
Subscribe to our newsletter:

VINE LEAVES PRESS

Enjoyed this book?
Go to vineleavespress.com to find more.
Subscribe to our newsletter.